FEAST OF FLAVOURS
from the Indonesian Kitchen

FEAST OF **FLAVOURS**

from the

Indonesian Kitchen

A STEP-BY-STEP CULINARY ADVENTURE

Heinz von Holzen

 **Marshall Cavendish**
Cuisine

Photographer: Heinz von Holzen
Designer: Rachel Chen

Published by Marshall Cavendish Cuisine
An imprint of Marshall Cavendish International
1 New Industrial Road, Singapore 536196

Other Marshall Cavendish Offices:

Marshall Cavendish Ltd. 119 Wardour Street, London W1F 0UW, UK • Marshall Cavendish Corporation.
99 White Plains Road, Tarrytown NY 10591-9001, USA • Marshall Cavendish International (Thailand) Co Ltd. 253 Asoke,
12th Flr, Sukhumvit 21 Road, Klongtoey Nua, Wattana, Bangkok 10110, Thailand • Marshall Cavendish (Malaysia) Sdn Bhd,
Times Subang, Lot 46, Subang Hi-Tech Industrial Park, Batu Tiga, 40000 Shah Alam, Selangor Darul Ehsan, Malaysia

Marshall Cavendish is a trademark of Times Publishing Limited

National Library Board Singapore Cataloguing in Publication Data

Holzen, Heinz von.
Feast of flavours from the Indonesian kitchen : a step-by-step culinary adventure / Heinz von Holzen. –
Singapore : Marshall Cavendish Cuisine, c2006.
p. cm. – (Feast of flavours)
Includes index.
ISBN : 978-981-261-302-8
ISBN : 981-261-302-1

1. Cookery, Indonesian. I. Title. II. Series: Feast of flavours

TX 724.5.I5
641.59598 – dc22   SLS2006019131

Printed in Singapore by Times Graphics Pte Ltd

Contents

ACKNOWLEDGEMENTS

I thank the many great people who helped and supported me
throughout the time when I was working on this book.

A very special thank you to Pak Bagus, our chef,
who passionately prepared each dish over and over again
to perfect the recipes and then again for the endless hours of photography.

My deepest gratitude goes to Mr Gaspare and the kitchen team
led by Mr Simon Tempe at the Gangga Island Resort & Spa
who introduced me to the many secrets of the cuisine of northern Sulawesi.

I will always be appreciative of Mr Francis Wibowo,
the Operations Manager of the Santika Hotel Group in Indonesia,
who enabled me to spend an exceedingly educational week
at the hotel in Malang, East Java. During that week,
the Group's Executive Chef Thomas Handajo and Chef Ferry Jeremia Raranta
spared no effort in introducing me to the delicious flavours of East Java.

Finally, a very special thank you to the teams in Rumah Bali and Bumbu Bali
that continue to stay totally dedicated to all the great culinary ventures
we are working on. Thank you for your encouragement and assistance
as we strive to promote the magnificent flavours of the archipelago to the world.

Heinz von Holzen

COOKING TECHNIQUES

Indonesia's cooking techniques are very simple and vary little from that of other cultures and cuisines. The source of heat, in many homes, remains a simple wood fire, although in some modern homes, kerosene and gas stoves are used. Cooking vessels are also simple, made from sheet iron or aluminium. Very rarely, and for only very few dishes, is a wok used.

Indonesians mostly use very low heat in cooking, meaning that the dishes take a longer time to cook. The key in preparing Indonesian dishes lies in the mixing and blending of spices, and as such, it is important to use only fresh ingredients when preparing Indonesian dishes.

Blanching

Blanching is a basic cooking process used when preparing leafy vegetables such as water spinach, spinach or fern tips, or a pre-cooking process for green beans, cabbage and bean sprouts, etc. The ratio of water to vegetables must be ten to one (10:1). The water should be well salted and boiling rapidly before vegetables are added. Lower vegetables into rapidly boiling water and allow water to return to the boil, then drain, rinse quickly and plunge into cold water, which will stop the cooking process. This method guarantees that the chlorophyll-containing vitamins and mineral salts are retained in green vegetables.

Blanching can also be used to cleanse bones meant for a stock. Place well washed bones in cold water and bring to a slow boil. This opens the pores and allows the impurities to flow out.

Boiling and Simmering

When it comes to boiling or simmering, it is important to know whether the food item should begin in cold or hot liquid. Always add rice or noodles into rapidly boiling liquid, for instance, as this will prevent the rice or noodles from sticking together, and stir frequently when boiling.

Meats such as chicken or beef should be added to simmering liquid or stock. This closes the pores and prevents the meat juices from being leached out, which causes the meat to become dry. Do not cover the pot as this will intensify the heat, increase boiling motions and in the case of stocks, make them cloudy.

Steaming

Steaming is a very popular cooking method throughout Indonesia for meat, fish, rice, vegetables, sausages and sweet snacks. It is a very gentle cooking process and steamed food retains many nutrients and vitamins, while keeping a most pleasant appearance.

Whole ducks and chickens are often wrapped in banana leaves when steamed. This protects the surface of the meat from harsh steam and also allows the interior to cook more evenly.

To steam, bring water in a steamer to a rapid boil, then position a rack inside. Place a plate or bowl containing items to be steamed on top of rack and replace steamer cover. Indonesians use a traditional steamer basket which also adds a certain flavour and aroma to the steamed food. Add some lemon grass, ginger and galangal to the boiling liquid for enhanced fragrance.

Poaching

Poaching is suitable for such diverse food items as sausages, fish, eggs, dumplings and bananas. Heat liquid (water or stock) to 70–80°C (160–175°F), then add food to be poached. Do not cover as this would immediately increase the heat and with that, the liquid would start to boil and cause many of the proteins, vitamins and minerals to be discharged and result in a loss of flavour, colour and shape.

Deep-frying

Deep-frying is the most widely used cooking method throughout Indonesia, as it only requires a vessel to cook in and plenty of oil. If not done properly, however, deep-frying becomes a most unhealthy and fattening way of cooking. To deep-fry well, always use oil which is neutral in flavour and suitable for heating. Peanut, soy and corn oils are ideal. The ratio of oil to food should be ten to one (10:1). Never lower large quantities of food into the heated oil as this will rapidly cool down the oil, open the pores of the food being cooked and cause the food to absorb excess oil. Instead, heat oil to 160–180°C (325–350°F), then add small quantities of food, which must be very dry, and fry at increasing heat. Drain cooked items thoroughly—first on a draining rack, then on paper towels.

Sautéing or Pan-frying

This is a very quick and basic cooking method for tender cuts of meat or fish. Heat oil in a shallow frying pan to medium-high hotness, add meat or fish fillets, seal (sear) both sides and continue cooking until food is cooked through.

To avoid overcooking food, coat it with breadcrumbs or batter which acts as an insulator to keep the food from coming into direct contact with high heat. Avoid having the heat reduce considerably as this will cause the pores of the meat or fish to open and lead to a loss of liquid or juices and toughen the food.

Grilling or Broiling

This very popular cooking method is mostly used for the preparation of saté, chicken and fish. For saté and other tender cuts, which are always cooked over glowing charcoal, ensure that the fire is very low and the heat very high. This, in Indonesia, is achieved by vigorously fanning air into the fire using a sturdy, hand-held bamboo fan. The heat should be as high as possible so that the skewers of saté are slightly burnt, which will add the desired slightly bitter, smoky aftertaste.

For fish, start grilling over very high heat to seal (sear) the outside, then lower the heat to finish grilling. Avoid having meat juices drip into the fire as this will cause the flames to leap up and add a very unpleasant burnt flavour to the food.

Frequently baste foods with an oil-based basting liquid to prevent the food and spices from burning and, at the same time, to ensure that the flavours of the seasoning penetrate the meat.

Note: Combining 125 g (4^1/$_2$ oz / ^{1}/$_2$ cup) spice paste (see pg 9–10) and 125 ml (4 fl oz / ^{1}/$_2$ cup) oil makes a delicious basting liquid. Use the Balinese Seafood Spice Paste for seafood, East Javanese Red Spice Paste for beef and lamb and the East Javanese Yellow Spice Paste for chicken.

Roasting

Roasting is usually done to cook whole ducks and chickens or, as on the island of Bali, whole pigs. Traditionally, roasting in Indonesia is done on a spit over an open fire when food is wrapped in various kinds of leaves, then buried under hot charcoal. In the modern kitchen, use a regular convection oven. For the first 15–20 minutes, roast at high heat or 180–200°C (350–400°F), then reduce the heat to 150–180°C (300–350°F). Frequently baste food with an oil-based basting liquid.

Braising or Glazing

This cooking method is more for secondary or tough cuts of meat, chicken and duck. Begin by heating oil in a heavy pan, then add meat and seal (sear) both sides, stirring frequently until the colour changes. Add all the spices and solid ingredients and sauté for a few minutes more. Finally, add liquid and braise meat over low heat until done. Stewing is very much similar to braising, except that lower heat is used. Note the following points for a successful braised or stewed dish:

1. Always use a stew pan, which is wide and shallow, and not a pot.
2. Always use cheap, secondary cuts such as brisket, shoulder or neck. Avoid using tender cuts because they cook too quickly and do not allow the sauce to develop a rich, meaty flavour.
3. The ratio of meat to liquid should be two to one (2:1) when liquid is added the first time. Keep liquid level as low as possible and regularly top up with small amounts as liquid evaporates during cooking; never add a large amount at once. This ensures that the sauce at the end will have the right, thickened consistency and the meat will have a shiny coating.
4. Never cover the pan when stewing.
5. Do not cook stews from start to finish in one go. Stew for about an hour or until meat is 75 per cent cooked, then remove from heat and leave to cool before refrigerating until the dish is required. Finally, reheat the stew and simmer until meat is tender, then season to taste and serve.

BASIC RECIPES

Balinese Seafood Spice Paste
(*Bumbu Ikan*)

Ingredients

Red chillies	450 g (1 lb), halved, seeded and sliced
Garlic	50 g (2 oz), peeled and sliced
Shallots	225 g (7½ oz), peeled and sliced
Turmeric	175 g (6 oz), peeled and sliced
Ginger	100 g (3½ oz), peeled and sliced
Candlenuts	125 g (4½ oz)
Tomatoes	200 g (7 oz), halved and seeded
Coriander seeds	2 Tbsp, crushed
Dried prawn (shrimp) paste (*terasi*)	2 Tbsp, roasted
Coconut or vegetable oil	150 ml (5 fl oz)
Tamarind pulp	2½ Tbsp
Salam leaves	3
Lemon grass	2 stalks, bruised
Salt	¾ Tbsp
Water	250 ml (8 fl oz / 1 cup)

Method

- Combine all ingredients except tamarind pulp, *salam* leaves, lemon grass, salt and water, in a stone mortar or blender (processor) and grind coarsely.
- Transfer ground ingredients to a heavy saucepan, add remaining ingredients and simmer over medium heat for about 1 hour or until all the liquid has evaporated and paste is golden in colour.
- Leave to cool completely before using or storing.

Northern Sulawesi Five-spice Paste
(*Bumbu Manado*)

Ingredients

Shallots	250 g (9 oz), peeled and sliced
Garlic	120 g (4 oz), peeled and sliced
Ginger	120 g (4 oz), peeled and sliced
Candlenuts	200 g (7 oz)
Bird's eye chillies	10–20, sliced
Lemon grass	3 stalks, bruised and finely sliced
Vegetable oil	150 ml (5 fl oz)
Water	125 ml (4 fl oz / ½ cup)
Salt	a pinch

Method

- Combine all ingredients, except oil, water and salt, in a stone mortar or blender (processor) and grind into a fine paste.
- Heat oil in a heavy saucepan, then add paste, water and salt. Bring to the boil and simmer until all the liquid has evaporated and paste is shiny.
- Leave to cool completely before using or storing.

Note: The people of northern Sulawesi would use substantially more chillies than indicated in this recipe, making their dishes fiery hot. The clean, crisp flavours of this spice paste is delicious when used with pork, chicken and seafood.

East Javanese Red Spice Paste
(*Bumbu Merah*)

Ingredients

Vegetable oil	4 Tbsp
Shallots	80 g (3 oz), peeled and sliced
Garlic	60 g (2 oz), peeled and sliced
Red chillies	200 g (7 oz), halved, seeded and sliced
Bird's eye chillies	40 g (1¼ oz)
Ginger	20 g (¾ oz), peeled and sliced
Galangal (*laos*)	20 g (¾ oz), peeled and sliced
Tomatoes	200 g (7 oz), peeled, halved, seeded and sliced
Salt	to taste
Ground white pepper	to taste
Lime juice	to taste

Method

- Heat oil in a heavy saucepan. Add shallots, garlic, chillies, ginger and galangal. Sauté over medium–low heat for 5 minutes or until ingredients are softened.
- Add tomatoes and sauté for 1 minute more, then remove from heat and leave to cool.
- Place sautéed ingredients in a stone mortar or blender (processor) and grind into a very fine paste.
- Season to taste with remaining ingredients, then use as required or store.

East Javanese Yellow Spice Paste (*Bumbu Kuning*)

Ingredients

Shallots	180 g (6 oz), peeled and sliced
Garlic	120 g (4 oz), peeled and sliced
Red chillies	160 g (5¹/₂ oz), halved, seeded and sliced
Turmeric	140 g (5 oz), peeled and sliced
Ginger	40 g (1¹/₄ oz), peeled and sliced
Galangal (*laos*)	40 g (1¹/₄ oz), peeled and sliced
Candlenuts	140 g (5 oz)
Lemon grass	5 stalks, bruised and finely sliced
Coriander seeds	4 Tbsp, roasted and crushed
Cumin seeds	1 Tbsp
Sweet soy sauce (*kecap manis*)	4 Tbsp
Chopped palm sugar	2 Tbsp
Vegetable oil	3 Tbsp
Chicken stock	500 ml (16 fl oz / 2 cups)
Salt	1¹/₂ Tbsp

Method

- Combine all ingredients, except oil, stock and salt, in a stone mortar or blender (processor) and grind coarsely.
- Transfer ground ingredients to a heavy saucepan, add oil and sauté over medium heat for 2 minutes or until fragrant.
- Add stock and simmer over low heat for about 30 minutes or until all the liquid has evaporated and paste is golden in colour. Season with salt.
- Leave to cool completely before using or storing.

Note: Each of the two East Javanese recipes yields about 500 g (1 lb 1¹/₂ oz / 2 cups) spice paste, which is sufficient for preparing about three recipes in this book. To store leftover paste, distribute it evenly among the cavities of an ice cube tray, packing in tightly, and freeze. Stored this way, the spice paste will keep for months. The red paste, in particular, can be used as a condiment to fried rice or noodles or as a marinade for saté ingredients, whether meat or vegetables. Once grilled, the red spice paste is remarkably tasty.

Coarsely grind all ingredients, except oil, stock and salt.

Sauté ground ingredients until fragrant, then add stock and simmer.

When stock has evaporated and paste is golden, season with salt.

Nasi Goreng Sauce (*Sambal Tomat*)

Ingredients

Vegetable oil	150 ml (5 fl oz)
Shallots	200 g (7 oz), peeled and sliced
Garlic	100 g (3¹/₂ oz), peeled and sliced
Red chillies	375 g (12¹/₂ oz), seeded and sliced
Bird's eye chillies	375 g (12¹/₂ oz), whole
Salam leaves	4
Dried prawn (shrimp) paste (*terasi*)	1¹/₂ Tbsp, roasted
Palm sugar	75 g (2¹/₂ oz), chopped
Tomatoes	500 g (1 lb 1¹/₂ oz), peeled and seeded
Salt	to taste
Lime juice	1 Tbsp or more to taste

Method

- Heat oil in heavy saucepan. Add shallots and garlic and sauté until golden.
- Add chillies and *salam* leaves and sauté until chillies are soft.
- Add prawn paste and palm sugar and continue to sauté until sugar caramelises.
- Add tomatoes and sauté until soft, then remove from heat and set aside to cool completely.
- Grind paste coarsely in a stone mortar or pulse in a blender (processor) for a similar effect.
- Season and adjust to taste with salt and lime juice.

Spiced Tomato Sauce (*Sambal Lado*)

Ingredients

Vegetable oil	2 Tbsp
Red chillies	100 g (3¹/₂ oz), halved, seeded and sliced
Shallots	40 g (1¹/₄ oz), peeled and sliced
Dried prawn (shrimp) paste (*terasi*)	¹/₂ tsp, roasted
Tomatoes	150 g (5 oz), peeled, halved, seeded and diced
Salt	to taste
Crushed black pepper	to taste

Method

- Combine all ingredients, except tomatoes, salt and pepper, in a stone mortar or blender (processor) and grind into a very fine paste.
- Add paste to a heated saucepan and sauté over medium heat until fragrant.
- Add tomatoes and sauté until soft, then season to taste and remove from heat.

Note: This sauce is delicious with grilled fish and meats.

Chicken or Beef Stock
(Kaldu Ayam dan Kaldu Sapi)

Ingredients

Chicken or beef bones	3 kg (6 lb 9 oz), trimmed of excess skin and fat and cut into walnut-size pieces
Vegetable oil	3 Tbsp
Shallots	200 g (7 oz), peeled and sliced
Garlic	100 g (3¹/₂ oz), peeled and sliced
Leeks	75 g (2¹/₂ oz), use only white parts, sliced
Celery stalks	75 g (2¹/₂ oz), sliced
Red chillies	3, bruised
Bird's eye chillies	5–7, bruised, use according to taste
Lemon grass	4 stalks, bruised
Kaffir lime leaves	5, bruised
Salam leaves	5
Coriander seeds	2 Tbsp, roasted and crushed
Black peppercorns	2 Tbsp, crushed
Cloves	8, crushed

Method

- Rinse bones until water runs clear, then drain and place in a stockpot.
- Add cold water until bones are submerged, then bring to the boil over high heat.
- Drain bones and discard liquid. Rinse bones again before placing in a larger stockpot.
- Add 3 times as much water as there are bones and bring to the boil, then reduce heat and simmer. Regularly skim off scum as it accumulates at the surface.
- In a saucepan, heat oil, add shallots and garlic and sauté over medium heat for 2 minutes.
- Add leeks, celery, chillies, lemon grass and kaffir lime and *salam* leaves. Sauté for 2 minutes more.
- Add 500 ml (16 fl oz / 2 cups) water and all remaining ingredients. Bring to the boil, then add to stock.
- Simmer stock for 5–6 hours over very low heat. Continue to regularly skim off scum.
- Strain and leave to cool before use or storing. If stock is meant for freezing, reduce it to a syrupy consistency over medium heat first; this creates a stock concentrate. Store cooled concentrate in ice cube trays and, once frozen, you will have great-tasting, home-made stock cubes.

Note: For variation, use a mixture of chicken and beef bones for this recipe. A carefully prepared stock is essential to any quality soup or sauce. Stocks must always be cooked slowly and do not cover the pot during cooking. Covering the pot will increase the heat and cause the stock to boil, which makes the stock cloudy.

Vegetable Stock (Kuah Sayur)

Ingredients

Vegetable oil	2 Tbsp
Shallots	75 g (2¹/₂ oz), peeled and sliced
Garlic	50 g (2 oz), peeled and sliced
Vegetable spice paste (see pg 19)	125 g (4¹/₂ oz)
Leek	75 g (2¹/₂ oz), sliced
Celery	75 g (2¹/₂ oz), use both stems and leaves, sliced
Cabbage	75 g (2¹/₂ oz), sliced
Spring onions (scallions)	100 g (3¹/₂ oz), sliced
Tomatoes	300 g (10 oz), diced
Red chilli	1, bruised
Bird's eye chillies	2, bruised
Water	2 litres (64 fl oz / 8 cups)
Lemon grass	2 stalks, bruised
Kaffir lime leaves	2, bruised
Coriander seeds	1 tsp, crushed
White peppercorns	¹/₂ tsp, crushed

Method

- Heat oil in a heavy saucepan. Add shallots and garlic and sauté until fragrant.
- Add spice paste and sauté until shallots and garlic are evenly coated and paste is fragrant.
- Add all the vegetables, tomatoes and chillies. Continue to sauté over medium–high heat until they are soft.
- Add all remaining ingredients. Bring to the boil and simmer over medium heat for 2 hours.
- Pass stock through a sieve, pressing on vegetables to extract as much liquid and flavour as possible. Alternatively, use a clean piece of cloth and squeeze vegetables by hand.

COOKING UTENSILS

Mortar and Pestle or Stone Grinder
By far the most important utensil, this is used for grinding, crushing and making spice pastes that are so central to the flavours of Indonesia. Choose a mortar that is slightly curved, heavy, sturdy and roughly textured. If available, purchase a mortar and pestle carved from volcanic rock because it is harder and, hence, more durable. This is because many spices are hard and require considerable force to grind by hand.

Food Processor or Meat Grinder
Most spice mixtures can be ground or better chopped in one of these kitchen aids. Especially during ceremonies, when meals for the whole village are prepared, the villagers often replace the heavy stone mortar set on the ground with a meat grinder. If using a blender (processor), the ingredients should be roughly chopped first and a little oil and water should be added while blending.

Pots and Pans
It is worthwhile to invest in good quality stainless steel or even copper pans. These will withstand years of reasonable usage, as well as remain hygenic and resistant to the corrosive action of certain foods and cleaning agents. They also will not impart an odour, colour or taste to the food. Stainless steel or copper pans distribute heat much more evenly and are less prone to hot spots, which cause food to stick and burn.

Several pots and pans, consisting of a basic range, are recommended. They are a 10–15-litre (2¹/2–4-gallon) stockpot; a stew pan; a shallow sauté or frying pan; a medium-sized pot; and finally, a perforated insert which can be placed inside the pot so that food can be steamed.

Rice Cooker
Because of the amount of rice Indonesians eat and the number of people cooked for, many households now use an electric rice cooker. A heavy saucepan with a perforated insert and a tight-fitting lid will work just as well.

Cutting Board or Chopping Block
Often meats or fish used in Indonesian cooking can be tough or very dry. This is why they are often minced and to do so easily, a heavy chopping board is useful. It is a good idea for sanitation reasons not to use one board for all tasks. Instead, have several differently coloured boards, one each for fish, meat, vegetables and fruit.

Grater and Shredder
A high quality stainless steel grater or shredder is useful for the grating of vegetables, coconuts, nutmeg or lime zest.

Measuring Spoons, Ladles and Scales
All recipes in this book are based on metric measures and it is recommended that the recipes are followed accurately. As such, it ideal to get an electronic scale with a range from 1 g to 2 kg (¹/30 oz to 4 lb 6 oz) and a set of stainless steel measuring spoons and ladles. It is absolutely essential that all basic recipes, such as the spice pastes and spiced tomato sauce, are followed faithfully for the consistent outcome of dishes.

WEIGHTS & MEASURES

Quantities for this book are given in Metric and American (spoon and cup) measures. Standard spoon and cup measurements used are:
1 teaspoon = 5 ml, 1 dessertspoon = 10 ml, 1 tablespoon = 15 ml, 1 cup = 250 ml. All measures are level unless otherwise stated.

LIQUID AND VOLUME MEASURES

Metric	Imperial	American
5 ml	$1/6$ fl oz	1 teaspoon
10 ml	$1/3$ fl oz	1 dessertspoon
15 ml	$1/2$ fl oz	1 tablespoon
60 ml	2 fl oz	$1/4$ cup (4 tablespoons)
85 ml	$2^1/2$ fl oz	$1/3$ cup
90 ml	3 fl oz	$3/8$ cup (6 tablespoons)
125 ml	4 fl oz	$1/2$ cup
180 ml	6 fl oz	$3/4$ cup
250 ml	8 fl oz	1 cup
300 ml	10 fl oz ($1/2$ pint)	$1^1/4$ cup
375 ml	12 fl oz	$1^1/2$ cup
435 ml	14 fl oz	$1^3/4$ cup
500 ml	16 fl oz	2 cups
625 ml	20 fl oz (1 pint)	$2^1/2$ cups
750 ml	24 fl oz ($1^1/5$ pint)	3 cups
1 litre	32 fl oz ($1^3/5$ pint)	4 cups
1.25 litres	40 fl oz (2 pints)	5 cups
1.5 litres	48 fl oz ($2^2/5$ pints)	6 cups
2.5 litres	80 fl oz (4 pints)	10 cups

OVEN TEMPERATURE

	°C	°F	Gas
Regulo			
Very slow	120	250	1
Slow	150	300	2
Moderately slow	160	325	3
Moderate	180	350	4
Moderately hot	190/200	370/400	5/6
Hot	210/220	410/440	6/7
Very hot	230	450	8
Super hot	250/290	475/550	9/10

ABBREVIATION

Tbsp	tablespoon
tsp	teaspoon
kg	kilogram
g	gram
l	litres
ml	millilitres

DRY MEASURES

Metric	Imperial
30 g	1 oz
45 g	$1^1/2$ oz
55 g	2 oz
70 g	$2^1/2$ oz
85 g	3 oz
100 g	$3^1/2$ oz
110 g	4 oz
125 g	$4^1/2$ oz
140 g	5 oz
280 g	10 oz
450 g	16 oz (1 lb)
500 g	1 lb, $1^1/2$ oz
700 g	$1^1/2$ lb
800 g	$1^3/4$ lb
1 kg	2 lb, 3 oz
1.5 kg	3 lb, $4^1/2$ oz
2 kg	4 lb, 6 oz

LENGTH

Metric	Imperial
0.5 cm	$1/4$ in
1 cm	$1/2$ in
1.5 cm	$3/4$ in
2.5 cm	1 in

Golden Vegetable Pickle (*Acar Kuning*)

Sweetcorn Patties (*Perkedel Jagung*)

Five-spice Pumpkin Braised in Coconut Milk (*Sambiki Santan*)

Vegetable and Bean Curd Stew (*Sambal Kerecek*)

Fried Bean Curd with Turmeric Sauce (*Tahu Kalas*)

Grilled Aubergines and Soy Bean Cake in Peanut Sauce (*Pecel Terong*)

VEGETABLES

Sauté ground spice paste ingredients with lemon grass for 2 minutes or until fragrant before adding stock.

Add blanched vegetables, peanuts, shallots, chillies and cucumber when stock has reduced by half.

When solid ingredients and spice paste are well mixed, add sugar, coconut milk and vinegar and simmer until sauce is slightly thickened.

S t e p - B y - S t e p

GOLDEN VEGETABLE PICKLE *(ACAR KUNING)*

In northern Sulawesi, this delightful and tasty vegetable dish is often served with seafood or pork dishes and generous helpings of rice.

Ingredients

Bamboo shoots	200 g (7 oz), cleaned and finely sliced
Green (French) beans	50 g (2 oz), sliced
Carrots	50 g (2 oz), peeled and finely sliced
Raw skinned peanuts	100 g (3½ oz)
Shallots	50 g (2 oz), peeled and left whole
Bird's eye chillies	15 g (½ oz), left whole
Cucumber	50 g (2 oz), halved, cored and sliced
Sugar	50 g (2 oz)
Coconut milk	175 ml (6 fl oz)
Rice vinegar	2 Tbsp
Salt	to taste

Spice Paste

Shallots	50 g (2 oz), peeled and sliced
Garlic	30 g (1 oz), peeled and sliced
Turmeric	20 g (¾ oz), peeled and sliced
Ginger	20 g (¾ oz), peeled and sliced
Vegetable oil	3 Tbsp
Lemon grass	2 stalks, bruised and knotted
Vegetable or chicken stock (see pg 11)	200 ml (6½ fl oz)

Method

- Blanch bamboo shoots for 1 minute, plunge into ice water to cool and drain. Repeat with beans and carrots.
- Prepare spice paste. Combine all ingredients, except oil, lemon grass and stock, in a stone mortar or blender (processor). Grind into a very fine paste.
- Heat oil in a heavy saucepan. Add spice paste and lemon grass. Sauté over low heat for 2 minutes or until fragrant.

- Add stock, stir through and simmer until half the liquid has evaporated.
- Add blanched vegetables, peanuts, shallots, chillies and cucumber. Gently mix in ingredients until they are evenly coated with spice paste.
- Add sugar, coconut milk and vinegar. Stir through and return to the boil, then simmer until sauce is slightly thickened.

- Season to taste with salt. Remove from heat and leave to cool; this dish as with most food in northern Sulawesi is eaten at room temperature.

SWEETCORN PATTIES
(PERKEDEL JAGUNG)

Crisp and light, these patties make a delightful snack or a charming addition to a rice-based meal.

Ingredients

Corn kernels	600 g (1 lb 5 oz)
Vegetable spice paste*	2 Tbsp
Plain (all-purpose) flour	2 Tbsp
Egg	1
Roughly chopped celery leaves	2 Tbsp
Salt	a pinch or to taste
Ground white pepper	a pinch
Cooking oil for deep-frying	

*Vegetable Spice Paste

Red chillies	50 g (2 oz), large, halved, seeded and sliced
Bird's eye chillies	2–3, finely sliced
Shallots	20 g (³/₄ oz), peeled and sliced
Garlic	20 g (³/₄ oz), peeled and sliced
Turmeric	20 g (³/₄ oz), peeled and sliced
Galangal (laos)	20 g (³/₄ oz), peeled and sliced
Candlenuts	20 g (³/₄ oz), roasted
Coriander seeds	¹/₂ tsp
Ground white pepper	¹/₄ tsp
Dried prawn (shrimp) paste (terasi)	¹/₂ tsp, roasted
Salt	¹/₂ tsp
Vegetable oil	3 Tbsp

Step-By-Step

Place fresh corn kernels in a stone mortar and grind coarsely before adding other ingredients.

Add all remaining ingredients, except the oil for deep-frying, and grind into a smooth paste.

Deep-fry corn patties in moderate–hot oil until golden before removing to drain on paper towels.

Method

- Prepare spice paste. Combine all ingredients, except oil, in a stone mortar or blender (processor) and grind coarsely.
- Heat oil in heavy saucepan. Add ground spices and sauté over medium heat until fragrant.
- Remove from heat and leave to cool thoroughly before using or storing for future use.

- Place corn in a stone mortar and grind coarsely with a pestle.
- Add all remaining ingredients, except oil, and grind into a smooth paste. Adjust seasoning to taste, if necessary.
- Shape 1 rounded (heaped) Tbsp of mixture into a patty and set aside. Repeat until mixture is used up.

- Deep-fry patties in moderate–hot oil until golden. Remove and place on paper towels to drain excess oil.
- Serve warm, with dipping sauce of choice on the side, if desired.

FIVE-SPICE PUMPKIN BRAISED IN COCONUT MILK
(SAMBIKI SANTAN)

Simple to prepare, this dish of braised pumpkin is rich with coconut milk and mildly spicy. Paired with plain, steamed rice, it makes a heartwarming meal.

Ingredients

Shallots	50 g (2 oz), peeled and sliced
Ginger	15 g (1/2 oz), peeled and sliced
Vegetable oil	3 Tbsp
Vegetable or chicken stock (see pg 11)	150 ml (5 fl oz)
Pumpkin	600 g (1 lb 5 oz), peeled and cubed
Screwpine (*pandan*) leaf	1, sliced
Turmeric leaf	1, sliced
Kaffir lime leaves	3, bruised
Lemon grass	1 stalk, bruised and knotted
Bird's eye chillies	10, seeded if desired
Coconut milk	350 ml (11 1/2 fl oz)
Lemon basil	10 g (1/3 oz), sliced
Spring onions (scallions)	75 g (2 1/2 oz), sliced
Salt	to taste

Heat 3 Tbsp oil and sauté ground shallots and ginger over medium heat until fragrant. Add 3 Tbsp stock to prevent sticking.

When pumpkin cubes are evenly coated with spice paste, add all remaining ingredients, except lemon basil, spring onions and salt.

Simmer pumpkin cubes in coconut milk until nearly soft before adding lemon basil and spring onions. Lastly, season to taste with salt.

Method

- Combine shallots and ginger in a stone mortar and grind into a very fine paste.
- Heat oil in a saucepan. Add paste and 3 Tbsp of stock and sauté over medium heat until fragrant.
- Add pumpkin cubes and stir until they are evenly coated with spice paste.
- Add all remaining ingredients, except lemon basil, spring onions and salt. Bring to the boil, reduce heat and simmer until pumpkin is almost soft.
- Add lemon basil and spring onions and simmer 2 minutes more.
- Season to taste with salt, then dish out and serve.

Heat 3 Tbsp oil and sauté all spice paste ingredients until fragrant before transferring to a stone mortar or blender (processor) to grind.

When sautéed ingredients have cooled, transfer them to a stone mortar and grind into a fine paste.

Add beef skin, fried bean curd and cluster beans to sauce and bring to the boil, then simmer until sauce is slightly thickened. Season to taste and serve.

Step-By-Step

VEGETABLE AND BEAN CURD STEW (SAMBAL KERECEK)

This slightly sweet dish makes a great-tasting and nourishing vegetarian meal when served with plain, steamed rice.

Ingredients

Vegetable oil	1 Tbsp
Palm sugar	1 Tbsp
Oyster sauce	1 Tbsp
Sweet soy sauce (*kecap manis*)	2 Tbsp
Sugar	1/4 tsp
Chicken stock (see pg 11)	125 ml (4 fl oz / 1/2 cup)
Coconut cream	125 ml (4 fl oz / 1/2 cup)
Firm bean curd	300 g (10 oz), sliced and fried for 2 minutes or until golden
Dried beef skin	300 g (10 oz), boiled in beef stock until very soft, left to cool in stock and sliced
Twisted cluster beans (*peteh*)	25 g (1 oz)
Salt	a pinch or to taste

Spice Paste

Vegetable oil	3 Tbsp
Garlic	40 g (1 1/4 oz), peeled and sliced
Shallots	60 g (2 oz), peeled and sliced
Red chillies	100 g (3 1/2 oz), halved, seeded and sliced
Ginger	10 g (1/3 oz), peeled and sliced
Galangal (*laos*)	10 g (1/3 oz), peeled and sliced
Dried prawn (shrimp) paste (*terasi*)	1 Tbsp, roasted
Palm sugar	1 Tbsp

Method

- Prepare spice paste. Heat oil in a heavy saucepan. Add all ingredients and sauté over medium heat until spices are fragrant.
- Remove from heat and leave to cool, then transfer to a stone mortar or blender (processor). Grind into a fine paste.

- Heat 1 Tbsp oil in a heavy saucepan. Add spice paste and sauté over medium heat until fragrant.
- Add palm sugar, oyster and sweet soy sauces and sugar. Continue to sauté for 1 minute.
- Add stock and coconut cream and bring to the boil.

- Add bean curd, beef skin and cluster beans. Return to the boil and simmer until sauce is slightly thickened. Add a splash of extra stock, if sauce thickens too much and season to taste.
- Serve, garnished as desired with finely chopped kaffir lime leaves.

Evenly dust bean curd pieces with about 2 Tbsp rice flour, then deep-fry in medium–hot oil until golden and crispy.

Sauté spice paste until fragrant before adding *salam* and lime leaves, lemon grass, chillies and sauté until fragrant again.

Add deep-fried bean curd to sauce and simmer over very low heat for 2 minutes. Turn bean curd frequently and season sauce to taste.

Step-By-Step

FRIED BEAN CURD WITH TURMERIC SAUCE
(TAHU KALAS)

Fried bean curd in a spicy turmeric-infused, coconut-based sauce, this dish makes a great appetiser or a side dish in a more extensive Indonesian meal.

Ingredients

Vegetable oil	2 Tbsp
East Javanese yellow spice paste (see pg 10)	125 g (4½ oz)
Salam leaves	2
Kaffir lime leaves	2, bruised
Lemon grass	1 stalk, bruised
Bird's eye chillies	1–3, chopped
Celery	50 g (2 oz), sliced
Young leek	50 g (2 oz), sliced
Vegetable or chicken stock (see pg 11)	375 ml (12 fl oz)
Coconut cream	180 ml (6 fl oz)
Firm bean curd	4, each 100 g (3½ oz), dusted with rice flour and deep-fried
Salt	a pinch or to taste
Freshly crushed white pepper	a pinch or to taste

Method

- Heat oil in a saucepan. Add spice paste and sauté until fragrant.
- Add *salam* and kaffir lime leaves, lemon grass and bird's eye chillies. Sauté until fragrant.
- Add celery and leek and sauté for 1 minute.
- Add stock, bring to the boil and simmer for 1 minute before adding coconut cream. Return to the simmer.
- Add fried bean curd and simmer over very low heat for 2 minutes, turning bean curd frequently. Add a splash of stock if sauce thickens too much.
- Season to taste with salt and pepper, then switch off heat.
- Prepare some garnishing, if desired. Finely slice some leek, celery and red chilli so there is a handful of each and place in a mixing bowl. Toss with 1 Tbsp lime juice and 2 Tbsp vegetable oil until well mixed. Season to taste, if desired.
- Serve bean curd as desired and topped with garnishing ingredients, if using.

GRILLED AUBERGINES AND SOY BEAN CAKE IN PEANUT SAUCE (PECEL TERONG)

The different nutty flavours and textures of grilled aubergines, soy bean cake and peanuts blend together beautifully in this dish.

Ingredients

Aubergines (eggplants/brinjals)	400 g (13½ oz), halved lengthways
Salt	a pinch
Vegetable oil	4 Tbsp
Fermented soy bean cake (tempe)	200 g (7 oz), sliced and crisp-fried
Eggs	4, soft-boiled for 4 minutes or poached
Lemon basil for garnishing	

Peanut Sauce

Vegetable oil	3 Tbsp
Red chillies	80 g (3 oz), halved, seeded and sliced
Bird's eye chillies	3–5
Garlic	20 g (¾ oz), peeled and sliced
Shallots	30 g (1 oz), peeled and sliced
Ginger	10 g (⅓ oz), peeled and sliced
Candlenuts	30 g (1 oz), crushed
Grated palm sugar	1 Tbsp
Kaffir lime leaves	5, bruised
Raw peanuts	250 g (9 oz), with skins intact and deep-fried or roasted
Coconut cream	3 Tbsp
Tamarind juice	1 Tbsp

When grinding peanuts, gradually add coconut cream, then tamarind juice. Prepare about 500 ml (16 fl oz / 2 cups) water to add to sauce, but not all may be needed.

Rub aubergines with salt and vegetable oil, then set aside for 10 minutes before grilling.

Grill salted and oiled aubergine halves until they become soft and their skins come off easily.

Method

- Prepare peanut sauce. Heat oil in a heavy saucepan. Add all ingredients, except peanuts, coconut cream and tamarind juice. Sauté over medium heat for 5 minutes or until fragrant.
- Remove sautéed ingredients from heat and leave to cool completely, then place in a stone mortar or blender (processor) and grind into a fine paste.
- Add peanuts and continue to grind, gradually adding coconut cream, then tamarind juice and just enough water, into a smooth, creamy sauce.

- Transfer sauce to a heavy saucepan and bring to the boil, then reduce heat and simmer until sauce is slightly thickened. Add a splash of water should sauce thicken too much; it should be creamy and warm when served.
- Rub aubergines with salt and vegetable oil, then leave for 10 minutes.
- Grill aubergines over medium–hot charcoal or oven-grill them until they are soft and their skins come off easily. Another way of grilling is to place aubergines on a piece of wire mesh set over a gas hob.

- Prepare 4 individual serving plates. Spoon a generous amount of sauce onto the centre of each, then top with some fried soy bean cake, 2 aubergine halves and a soft-boiled or poached egg.
- Garnish as desired with lemon basil and serve.

Prawns Marinated with Lime and Basil (*Gon Udang*)

Tuna Salad with Green Mangoes (*Sambal Tapa*)

Grilled Fish with Tomatoes and Chillies (*Ikan Bakar Dabu-dabu*)

Prawns with Coconut Flesh (*Udang Kelapa*)

Hot and Sour Seafood Soup (*Ikan Asam Pedas*)

Crab in Turmeric Sauce (*Kepiting Kuning*)

Clams Braised in Spiced Coconut Milk (*Rendang Kerang*)

Grilled Fish in Banana Leaf (*Ikan Woku Daun*)

Clear Prawn and Soy Bean Cake Broth (*Pindang Tempe*)

This dish is similar to Latin American *ceviche* in that it does not require stove-top cooking, so use only the freshest seafood in preparing it.

Add lime juice to shelled prawns and mix well, then refrigerate for 30 minutes. Mix in lime halves for added fragrance, if desired.

Toss marinated prawns with prepared dressing only just before serving. Season to taste with salt and serve.

Note: This dish originated from Manado, in far north Indonesia, where it is eaten as a light snack accompanied by tapioca (cassava) roots that have been boiled in salted water with lemon grass. To counter the fieriness of bird's eye chillies, a glass of *saledo*, a brandy distilled from palm wine, is usually drunk.

PRAWNS MARINATED WITH LIME AND BASIL
(GON UDANG)

Instead of prawns (shrimps), finely sliced fish such as tuna, mackerel, mahi-mahi or snapper can be used for this light and refreshing dish.

Ingredients

Shelled prawns (shrimps)	600 g (1 lb 5 oz)
Lime juice	4 Tbsp
Salt	to taste

Dressing

Shallots	60 g (2 oz), peeled and sliced
Bird's eye chillies	5 g, finely sliced
Lemon basil leaves	10 g ($^1/_3$ oz), left whole or roughly chopped

Method

- Place prawns in a bowl and mix with lime juice, then refrigerate for 30 minutes.
- Prepare dressing. Combine all ingredients and mix well.
- Mix prawns with dressing just before serving and season to taste with salt.

TUNA SALAD WITH GREEN MANGOES (*SAMBAL TAPA*)

Although tamed, the green mango shreds still retain some tanginess and acidity which makes this dish a great appetiser.

Ingredients

Tuna steaks	4, each about 150 g (5 oz)
Green mangoes	2, about 200 g (7 oz), peeled and coarsely shredded
Salt	1 Tbsp
Shallots	50 g (2 oz), peeled and sliced
Coconut cream	125 ml (4 fl oz / ¹/₂ cup)

Seasoning

Salt	¹/₂ tsp
Freshly crushed black pepper	¹/₂ tsp
Lime juice	1 Tbsp

Garnishing

Finely chopped red chillies
Finely chopped kaffir lime
  leaves

Step-By-Step

Pan-fry or oven-grill seasoned tuna steaks until medium–well done, then set aside to cool before flaking.

Place shredded green mango in a bowl and add 1 Tbsp salt. Toss until well mixed and set aside for 10 minutes.

Toss mango, tuna, shallots and coconut cream together until well mixed. Mix in garnishing ingredients here for added flavour.

Method

- Rub tuna steaks with seasoning ingredients, then oven-grill or pan-fry over low heat until medium–well done.
- Remove cooked tuna and leave to cool to room temperature before flaking into small pieces.
- Place shredded mangoes in a bowl, add 1 Tbsp salt and mix well, then set aside for 10 minutes.

- Squeeze mango shreds for sour juices to discard, then rinse mango thoroughly under running water to remove salt.
- Drain shredded mango well and squeeze again until very dry.
- Combine tuna, mangoes, shallots and coconut cream in a large bowl. Toss until well mixed and adjust seasoning to taste with salt and pepper, if necessary.

- Transfer to a platter to serve or divide among individual serving plates, then garnish as desired.

GRILLED FISH WITH TOMATOES AND CHILLIES
(IKAN BAKAR DABU-DABU)

Instead of using a whole fish, this recipe can also be prepared with firm fish fillets, such as snapper, mahi-mahi or mackerel. Use approximately 600 g (1 lb 5 oz) in place of whole fish.

Ingredients

Whole fish	4, each about 500 g (1 lb 1½ oz), use snapper or similar

Seasoning

Salt	to taste
Freshly crushed white pepper	¼ tsp
Lime juice	2 Tbsp
Vegetable oil	2 Tbsp + more for basting

Sauce

Tomatoes	200 g (7 oz), peeled, halved, seeded and diced
Bird's eye chillies	5–10, sliced, use more or less according to taste
Shallots	50 g (2 oz), peeled and sliced
Lime juice	2 Tbsp
Salt	a pinch
Vegetable oil	3 Tbsp

Step-By-Step

Rub fish with seasoning ingredients, then set aside in a cool place or refrigerate for 30 minutes. Be sure to rub seasoning into the slits as well.

To prepare sauce, combine all ingredients in a bowl and mix well, then set aside for 30 minutes so flavours can infuse.

Method
- Use a sharp knife to make 4 slits, each about 2-cm (1-in) deep, on both sides of fish. This not only helps the seasoning to better penetrate the fish, but also helps the fish to cook more evenly.
- Rub fish with seasoning ingredients, then refrigerate or leave in a cool place for 30 minutes to marinate.
- Meanwhile, prepare sauce. Combine all ingredients and mix well, then set aside in a cool place for 30 minutes.
- Grill (broil) fish over hot charcoal for a few minutes on each side, basting frequently with vegetable oil. This prevents the fish from sticking to the grill and helps the seasoning to penetrate the fish. Alternatively, oven-grill until cooked.
- Remove grilled fish and place on a serving platter. Serve with sauce spooned on top or on the side.

Mix shelled prawns with lime juice, 2 Tbsp oil and salt and pepper to taste, then set aside for 30 minutes.

For added flavour and aroma, add kaffir lime and turmeric leaves, as well as lemon grass to pan when sautéing spice paste.

When spice paste is fragrant, add prawns, coconut and remaining stock. Continue to sauté until prawns are cooked and season to taste.

Step-By-Step

PRAWNS WITH COCONUT FLESH
(UDANG KELAPA)

The use of tender coconut flesh in this dish is unusual, and it helps to counter the spiciness of the bird's eye chillies.

Ingredients

Prawns (shrimps)	600 g (1 lb 5 oz), shelled and deveined
Lime juice	3 Tbsp
Vegetable oil	2 Tbsp
Salt	to taste
Freshly crushed white pepper	to taste
Chicken stock (see pg 11)	100 ml (3^1/$_2$ fl oz)
Kaffir lime leaves	4, bruised
Turmeric leaf	^{1}/$_2$, sliced
Lemon grass	2 stalks, bruised
Tender coconut flesh	200 g, sliced

Spice Paste

Shallots	70 g (2^1/$_2$ oz), peeled and sliced
Ginger	30 g (1 oz), peeled and sliced
Turmeric	30 g (1 oz), peeled and sliced
Bird's eye chillies	15 g (^{1}/$_2$ oz), sliced
Vegetable oil	3 Tbsp

Method

- Place prawns in a mixing bowl. Add lime juice, oil and salt and pepper to taste. Mix well and refrigerate or leave in a cool place for 30 minutes.
- Meanwhile, prepare spice paste. Combine all ingredients, except oil, in a stone mortar or blender (processor) and grind into a fine paste.

- Heat oil in a saucepan and add spice paste. Sauté over low heat until fragrant, adding 3 Tbsp stock during sautéing to prevent sticking.
- Add prawns and all remaining ingredients. Increase heat to medium and sauté until prawns are cooked.

- Adjust seasoning to taste before dishing out to serve. Garnish, if desired, with finely chopped red chillies and kaffir lime leaves.

Season fish with salt and pepper, then refrigerate or set aside in a cool place until needed. Mix in a few lime halves to remove any fishiness.

Sauté all spice mix ingredients in 3 Tbsp oil for 2 minutes or until fragrant.

Add fish pieces to stock mixture and return to a simmer. Poach fish at just below 80°C (180°F) for 5 minutes.

S
t
e
p
-
B
y
-
S
t
e
p

HOT AND SOUR SEAFOOD SOUP
(IKAN ASAM PEDAS)

This recipe can be prepared with assorted seafood instead of a whole fish. If using assorted seafood, prepare about 800 g (1¾ lb). Use firm fish fillets, prawns (shrimps), clams, etc.

Ingredients

Whole fish	1, about 1 kg (2 lb 3 oz), cleaned and cut into roughly equal slices, use red mullet, snapper or mackerel
Salt	to taste
Freshly crushed black pepper	to taste
Chicken stock (see pg 11)	1 litre (32 fl oz / 4 cups)
Tomatoes	4, medium, skinned, seeded and cut into wedges
Salam leaves	2, finely sliced

Spice Mixture

Vegetable oil	3 Tbsp
Red chillies	60 g (2 oz), halved, seeded and sliced
Shallots	80 g (3 oz), peeled and sliced
Garlic	40 g (1¼ oz), peeled and sliced
Lemon grass	2 stalks, bruised and finely sliced
Galangal (*laos*)	30 g (1 oz), peeled and cut into fine strips
Turmeric	30 g (1 oz), peeled and finely sliced
Ginger	30 g (1 oz), peeled and finely sliced
Lemon basil	12 sprigs, roughly sliced
Blimbing (*belimbing*)	10, halved and sliced

Method

- Season fish with salt and pepper to taste, then refrigerate or set aside in a cool place until needed.
- Prepare spice mixture. Heat oil in a heavy saucepan. Add all ingredients and sauté over medium heat for 2 minutes or until fragrant.
- Season spice mixture to taste with salt and pepper, then add stock. Bring to the boil and simmer for 1 minute.
- Lower fish into stock mixture, return to a simmer and poach fish at just below 80°C (180°F) for 5 minutes.
- Carefully remove fish from saucepan and arrange in one large serving bowl or divide among individual serving ones.
- Finally, add tomatoes to soup and return to a simmer. Adjust seasoning to taste with more salt and pepper, if necessary.
- Ladle soup over fish, sprinkle *salam* leaves over to garnish and serve.

Cook crabs, one at a time, in 5 litres (8 pints / 20 cups) of heavily salted, boiling water. Add a few wedges of lime to remove any fishiness.

After boiling, plunge each crab in ice water for 5 minutes, then drain and dry well.

When crab pieces are evenly coated with spice paste, add stock and bring to the boil, then reduce heat and simmer for 1 minute.

Step-By-Step

CRAB IN TURMERIC SAUCE
(KEPITING KUNING)

To save time, replace spice paste in this recipe with 250 g (9 oz / 1 cup) Balinese Seafood Spice Paste on page 9.

Ingredients

Mud crabs	2 kg (4 lb 6 oz), large
Chicken stock (see pg 11)	750 ml (24 fl oz / 3 cups)
Tomatoes	4, peeled, seeded and sliced
Blimbing (*belimbing*)	2, sliced
Salt	to taste
Freshly crushed black pepper	to taste
Lime juice	

Spice Paste

Red chillies	150 g (5 oz), halved, seeded and sliced
Shallots	60 g (2 oz), peeled and sliced
Garlic	30 g (1 oz), peeled and sliced
Turmeric	60 g (2 oz), peeled and sliced
Ginger	30 g (1 oz), peeled and sliced
Candlenuts	40 g (1¼ oz)
Coriander seeds	1 tsp, roasted and crushed
Dried prawn (shrimp) paste (*terasi*)	1 tsp, roasted
Tamarind pulp	1 Tbsp, seeds discarded
Vegetable oil	4 Tbsp
Salam leaves	2
Kaffir lime leaves	2, bruised
Lemon grass	2 stalks, bruised

Method

- Bring 5 litres (8 pints / 20 cups) of heavily salted water to the boil.
- Cook crabs one at a time. With each addition, ensure that water returns to the boil and boil for 1 minute before removing.
- Plunge each boiled crab into ice water and leave to chill for 5 minutes, then drain and dry well.
- With each crab, break off pincers and crush shell evenly with a pestle or kitchen mallet. Dislodge top shell and rinse clean under running water. Quarter remaining body of crab.

- Prepare spice paste. Combine all ingredients, except *salam* and lime leaves and lemon grass, in a stone mortar or blender (processor) and grind into a fine paste.
- Transfer paste to a heavy saucepan and add all remaining ingredients. Place over medium heat and cook until paste is fragrant and takes on a golden colour.
- Add crab pieces and stir until they are evenly coated with spice paste.
- Add stock and bring to the boil, then reduce heat and simmer for 1 minute.

- Add tomatoes and blimbing. Mix well and return to the boil. Season to taste with salt and pepper and add a generous squeeze of lime juice.
- Dish out and garnish, if desired, with finely chopped kaffir lime leaves. Serve warm.

CLAMS BRAISED IN SPICED COCONUT MILK
(RENDANG KERANG)

This dish may require a bit more preparation than others, but the result is also that much more rewarding.

Ingredients

Clams	2 kg (4 lb 6 oz), scrubbed clean and washed
Chicken stock (see pg 11)	125 ml (4 fl oz / ½ cup)
Coconut milk	250 ml (8 fl oz / 1 cup)
Salam leaves	2
Turmeric leaf	1, bruised
Kaffir lime leaves	2, bruised
Ground nutmeg	a pinch
Lemon grass	2 stalks, bruised

Spice Paste

Vegetable oil	3 Tbsp
Shallots	80 g (3 oz), peeled and sliced
Garlic	50 g (2 oz), peeled and sliced
Turmeric	50 g (2 oz), peeled and sliced
Red chillies	100 g (3½ oz), halved seeded and sliced
Bird's eye chillies	4, sliced

Seasoning

Lime juice	1 Tbsp
Sugar	½ tsp
Salt	to taste

Step-By-Step

Buy clams that are tightly closed, which means that they are alive. To prepare clams for use, scrub shells clean and pull off beards.

When spice paste is fragrant, add clams and stir until they are evenly coated with the spice paste.

Add seasoning ingredients and adjust to taste after clams have opened up, which means that they are cooked.

Method

- Prepare spice paste. Combine all ingredients in a stone mortar or blender (processor) and grind into a fine paste.
- Transfer spice paste to a heavy saucepan and sauté over medium heat until fragrant.
- Increase heat, add clams and stir until they are evenly coated with spice paste.
- Add all remaining ingredients, except seasoning. Mix well and bring to the boil, then reduce heat and simmer until clams open, which indicates that they are cooked.
- Add seasoning ingredients and adjust to taste, then dish out and serve immediately. Garnish, if desired, with sprigs of lemon basil.

Whether using whole fish or fish fillets, rub all over with seasoning ingredients and refrigerate or set aside in a cool place for 30 minutes.

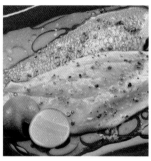

Place piece of fish, whether fillet or whole, on top of 1 rounded (heaped) Tbsp of spice paste on a banana leaf, then spoon more paste over.

Wrap fish tightly in banana leaf by folding in thirds lengthways, then secure with skewers or kitchen string.

GRILLED FISH IN BANANA LEAF
(IKAN WOKU DAUN)

The aroma of banana leaves, while subtle, imparts a certain freshness to this dish, which can also be prepared with smaller whole fish.

Ingredients

Fish fillets or whole fish	4, each about 350 g (12 oz)
Vegetable oil	3 Tbsp
Water or chicken stock (see pg 11)	3 Tbsp
Spring onions (scallions)	80 g (3 oz), sliced
Turmeric leaf	1, sliced
Kaffir lime leaves	3, finely chopped
Lemon basil	10 g (1/3 oz), sliced
Salt	to taste
Banana leaves	4, each 25 x 30 cm (10 x 12 in)

Seasoning

Salt	to taste
Freshly crushed white pepper	to taste
Lime juice	4 Tbsp
Vegetable oil	4 Tbsp

Spice Paste

Shallots	50 g (2 oz), peeled and sliced
Bird's eye chillies	10 g (1/3 oz), sliced
Ginger	15 g (1/2 oz), peeled and sliced
Candlenuts	50 g (2 oz), crushed
Turmeric	10 g (1/3 oz), peeled and sliced
Lemon grass	2 stalks, bruised and finely sliced

Method

- If using whole fish, gut and clean thoroughly, then use a sharp knife to make 4 slits on both sides of fish.
- Rub fish all over, including slits if using whole fish, with seasoning ingredients. Refrigerate for 30 minutes.
- Prepare spice paste. Combine all ingredients in a stone mortar or blender (processor) and grind into a fine paste.

- Heat oil in a saucepan. Add spice paste and sauté over low heat until fragrant, adding stock or water to prevent sticking.
- Add all remaining ingredients, except salt and banana leaves. Sauté for 1 minute or until well mixed.
- Remove from heat and leave to cool to room temperature, then season to taste with salt.

- Place 1 rounded (heaped) Tbsp spice mixture on the centre of each banana leaf. Place fish on top and cover fish with more spice paste.
- Wrap fish tightly in banana leaf and secure with skewers or kitchen string.
- Steam parcels for 7–10 minutes or until cooked through, then serve as desired.

To prepare stock, sauté prawn shells, shallots and leek over medium heat for 2 minutes before adding water.

Another way of grilling the spice skewers is to place them on a piece of wire mesh set over a gas hob. Remove when evenly browned.

Add soy bean cakes after stock, spice skewers, chillies and seasoning ingredients have simmered over low heat for 5 minutes.

Step-By-Step

CLEAR PRAWN AND SOY BEAN CAKE BROTH
(PINDANG TEMPE)

The flavour and crisp texture of the prawns (shrimps) make a great foil for the nuttiness of soy bean cakes.

Ingredients

Prawns (shrimps)	300 g (10 oz), medium
Fermented soy bean cakes (tempe)	300 g (10 oz)
Red chillies	120 g (4 oz), about 8 pieces
Bird's eye chillies	20 g ($^3/_4$ oz), bruised
Sweet soy sauce (kecap manis)	2 Tbsp
Ground white pepper	$^1/_4$ tsp
Sugar	$^1/_4$ tsp

Stock

Vegetable oil	2 Tbsp
Prawn (shrimp) shells	500 g (1 lb 1$^1/_2$ oz)
Shallots	200 g (7 oz), peeled and sliced
Leek	100 g (3$^1/_2$ oz), sliced, use white parts only
Water	1.5 litres (48 fl oz / 6 cups)

Spice Skewers

Ginger	4 pieces, each about 8 g ($^1/_4$ oz), peeled
Galangal (laos)	4 pieces, each about 8 g ($^1/_4$ oz), peeled
Turmeric	4 pieces, each about 8 g ($^1/_4$ oz), peeled
Lemon grass	4 pieces, each about 8 g ($^1/_4$ oz), use bulbous ends only
Bamboo skewers	4, pre-soaked
Garlic	8 cloves, peeled

Method

- Shell and devein prawns. Reserve shells and add to those for stock. Blanch shelled prawns for 1 minute, then drain and set aside until needed.
- Slice fermented soy bean cakes into desired serving-size pieces and set aside.
- Prepare stock. Heat oil in a heavy saucepan. Add prawn shells, shallots and leek. Sauté over medium heat for 2 minutes.
- Add water and bring to the boil, then reduce heat and simmer for 30 minutes.

- Strain stock into a clean saucepan, return to the boil and reduce until 1 litre (32 fl oz / 4 cups) liquid remains. Remove from heat and set aside.
- Prepare spice skewers. Bruise ginger, galangal, turmeric and lemon grass. Onto each skewer, thread 2 cloves of garlic and a piece of each remaining ingredient.
- Grill (broil) skewers over medium–hot charcoal or oven-grill them until evenly browned.

- Combine stock, spice skewers, chillies, sweet soy sauce, pepper and sugar in a pot or large saucepan. Bring to the boil and simmer over low heat for 5 minutes.
- Add soy bean cakes and simmer for 5 minutes, then add prawns and simmer for 2 minutes more.
- Remove from heat, dish out and serve.

Minced Duck Saté (*Sate Bebek Lilit*)

Chicken in Spiced Coconut Sauce (*Opor Ayam*)

Chicken with Tomato Sambal (*Ayam Rica-rica*)

Spiced Chicken Stew with Potatoes (*Semur Ayam*)

Mushrooms and Chicken in Banana Leaf (*Pepes Ayam Jamur*)

Spiced Chicken in Coconut Cream (*Ayam Tuturuga*)

Creamy Duck Curry (*Bebek Menyanyat*)

Mix together minced duck meat, all remaining ingredients and 4 Tbsp spice paste.

If desired, pinch a spiral pattern around the meat after moulding it onto one end of a skewer.

Repeat moulding meat onto skewers until ingredients are used up.

Step-By-Step

MINCED DUCK SATÉ
(SATE BEBEK LILIT)

A welcome variation from the usual beef, mutton or chicken saté, this recipe also works well with pork or game meat.

Ingredients

Minced duck meat	600 g (1 lb 5 oz)
Grated coconut	125 g (4$^{1}/_{2}$ oz)
Bird's eye chillies	4, finely chopped
Crisp-fried shallots	2 Tbsp
Crisp-fried garlic	1 Tbsp
Chopped palm sugar	1 tsp
Salt	a pinch
Freshly crushed black pepper	a pinch
Bamboo skewers or trimmed lemon grass stalks	

Spice Paste

Red chillies	60 g (2 oz), halved seeded and sliced
Shallots	60 g (2 oz), peeled and sliced
Garlic	30 g (1 oz), peeled
Galangal (laos)	20 g ($^{3}/_{4}$ oz), peeled and sliced
Turmeric	30 g (1 oz), peeled and sliced
Ginger	20 g ($^{3}/_{4}$ oz), peeled and sliced
Candlenuts	20 g ($^{3}/_{4}$ oz), crushed
Dried prawn (shrimp) paste (terasi)	$^{1}/_{4}$ tsp, roasted
Coriander seeds	$^{1}/_{4}$ tsp, crushed
Freshly crushed black pepper	a pinch
Grated nutmeg	a pinch
Cloves	2
Vegetable oil	3 Tbsp

Method

- Prepare spice paste. Combine all ingredients, except oil, in a stone mortar or blender (processor) and grind into a fine paste.
- Heat oil in a heavy saucepan. Add spice paste and sauté over low heat until fragrant and colour has changed.
- Remove from heat and set aside to cool completely before using or storing.

- Combine all ingredients, except skewers or lemon grass stalks, in a mixing bowl. Add 4 Tbsp spice paste and mix into a smooth paste.
- Mould 1 rounded (heaped) Tbsp mixture around one end of a bamboo skewer or the bulbous end of a lemon grass stalk. Repeat until ingredients are used up.

- Prepare a basting mixture. Mix 2 Tbsp spice paste with 2 Tbsp vegetable oil until well blended.
- Either grill prepared saté over very hot charcoal or oven-grill until golden brown, basting and turning frequently.

CHICKEN IN SPICED COCONUT SAUCE
(OPOR AYAM)

To save time, replace spice paste in this recipe with 190 g (6½ oz / ¾ cup) East Javanese Yellow Spice Paste (see pg 10). Finishing the sauce with lime juice helps to accentuate its complex blend of flavours.

Ingredients

Vegetable oil	2 Tbsp
Chicken thighs (legs)	600 g (1 lb 1½ oz), boned and cut into 2.5-cm (1-in) cubes
Chicken stock (see pg 11)	150 ml (5 fl oz)
Lemon grass	2 stalks, bruised
Salam leaves	2
Coconut cream	125 ml (4 fl oz / ½ cup)
Salt	to taste
Ground white pepper	to taste
Lime juice	

Spice Paste

Coriander seeds	1 Tbsp, roasted
Cumin seeds	1 tsp
White peppercorns	½ tsp
Candlenuts	25 g (1 oz), roasted and crushed
Galangal (*laos*)	30 g (1 oz), peeled and sliced
Shallots	60 g (2 oz), peeled and sliced
Garlic	30 g (1 oz), peeled and sliced
Palm sugar	15 g (½ oz), chopped

Step-By-Step

For added fragrance, add lemon grass and *salam* leaves when sautéing spice paste.

After adding stock, bring to the boil, then reduce heat to simmer for 3 minutes.

Add coconut cream, return to the boil and simmer for 2 minutes or until sauce thickens.

Method

- Prepare spice paste. Combine coriander, cumin and white peppercorns in a stone mortar and grind until very fine, then add all remaining ingredients and grind into a fine paste.
- Heat oil in heavy saucepan. Add spice paste and sauté until fragrant.
- Add chicken cubes and continue to sauté until they are evenly coated with spice paste and their colour has changed.
- Add stock, lemon grass and *salam* leaves. Bring to the boil, reduce heat and simmer over low heat for 3 minutes.
- Add coconut cream, return to the boil and simmer for 2 minutes more or until sauce thickens and chicken is tender.
- Season to taste with salt and pepper, then add a generous squeeze of lime juice before serving.
- Should sauce thicken too much during cooking, add splashes of stock to thin it down.

CHICKEN WITH TOMATO SAMBAL
(AYAM RICA-RICA)

This dish of tender chicken with an appetising sauce that is mildly spicy and tangy goes brilliantly with plain, steamed rice.

Ingredients

Spring chickens	4, each about 750 g (1 lb 10 oz), quartered
Salt	1 Tbsp
Freshly crushed black pepper	1/2 Tbsp
Lime juice	2 Tbsp
Vegetable oil	4 Tbsp
Chicken stock (see pg 11)	500 ml (16 fl oz / 2 cups)
Shallots	40 g (1 1/4 oz), peeled and chopped
Garlic	30 g (1 oz), peeled and chopped
Tomatoes	160 g (5 oz), peeled, halved, seeded and diced
Lemon basil	2 Tbsp, sliced
Lime juice	4 Tbsp
Sweet soy sauce (kecap manis)	2 Tbsp
Salt	a pinch or to taste
Freshly crushed black pepper	a pinch or to taste

Spice Paste

Red chillies	100 g (3 1/2 oz), halved, seeded and sliced
Bird's eye chillies	25 g (1 oz), sliced
Shallots	60 g (2 oz), peeled and sliced
Garlic	40 g (1 1/4 oz), peeled and sliced
Dried prawn (shrimp) paste (terasi)	1/2 Tbsp, roasted

Step-By-Step

Rub chicken pieces with 1 Tbsp salt, 1/2 Tbsp freshly crushed black pepper and 2 Tbsp lime juice, then leave for 30 minutes.

Sauté ground spice paste ingredients over medium heat until fragrant before adding chicken.

Bring to the boil after stirring in stock, then reduce heat and simmer, covered, until chicken is tender and most of the liquid has evaporated.

Method

- Season chicken pieces with salt, pepper and lime juice. Refrigerate or leave in a cool place for 30 minutes.
- Meanwhile, prepare spice paste. Combine all ingredients in a stone mortar or blender (processor) and grind into a very fine paste.

- Heat half the oil in a large, heavy saucepan and sauté spice paste over medium heat until fragrant.
- Add chicken pieces and sauté until they are evenly coated with spice paste.
- Stir in stock and bring to the boil, then reduce heat, cover and simmer until chicken is tender and most of the liquid has evaporated.

- Remove chicken from saucepan and keep warm, then add remaining oil to saucepan and heat.
- Add all remaining ingredients and sauté for 1 minute or until they are warmed through. Adjust seasoning to taste before serving.
- Garnish, if desired, with a sprig of lemon basil.

SPICED CHICKEN STEW WITH POTATOES
(SEMUR AYAM)

Aromatic from garlic, shallots and galangal, this sweetish dish is simple to prepare and made hearty by the fried potatoes.

Ingredients

Chicken thighs (legs)	800 g (1³/₄ lb), boned
Vegetable oil	3 Tbsp + enough for deep-frying
Garlic	20 g (³/₄ oz), peeled and sliced
Shallots	30 g (1 oz), peeled and sliced
Galangal (*laos*)	20 g (³/₄ oz), peeled, sliced and bruised
Chicken stock (see pg 11)	500 ml (16 fl oz / 2 cups)
Potatoes	200 g (7 oz), peeled, sliced and deep-fried until golden
Salt	a pinch or to taste
Ground white pepper	¹/₄ tsp or to taste

Seasoning

Sweet soy sauce (*kecap manis*)	3 Tbsp
Salty soy sauce (*kecap asin*)	2 Tbsp
Oyster sauce	1 Tbsp
Sweet chilli sauce	2 Tbsp

Garnishing

Crisp-fried shallots
Lime wedges
Finely chopped kaffir lime leaves

When garlic, shallots and galangal have been sautéed until fragrant, add seasoning ingredients of both soy sauces and oyster and sweet chilli sauces.

Add stock when the solid ingredients are evenly coated with seasoning ingredients and glazed.

Bring to the boil and simmer for 1 minute after adding stock, then add chicken and return to the boil.

Method

- Cut chicken thigh meat into 2.5-cm (1-in) cubes. Set aside.
- Heat sufficient oil for deep-frying chicken to 180°C (350°F), then fry for 1 minute. Remove and place on a wire rack to drain.
- Heat 3 Tbsp oil in heavy saucepan. Add garlic, shallots and galangal. Sauté over medium heat until fragrant.

- Add all seasoning ingredients and continue to sauté until solid ingredients are evenly coated and glazed.
- Add stock, bring to the boil and simmer for 1 minute, then add chicken and return to the boil.
- Reduce heat and simmer, stirring continuously, until chicken is tender.

- Remove chicken from sauce and keep warm, then reduce sauce to a syrupy consistency.
- Mix in fried potatoes and chicken. Season to taste with salt and pepper.
- Dish out, garnish as desired and serve.

Prepare spice paste by grinding all ingredients, except oil, into a very fine paste.

Place a *salam* leaf at the centre of each banana leaf wrapper and top with 2 Tbsp of chicken and mushroom mixture.

Secure the open ends of each parcel with cocktail sticks or skewers.

MUSHROOMS AND CHICKEN IN BANANA LEAF
(PEPES AYAM JAMUR)

Deeply aromatic and flavourful, these steamed parcels are equally delightful eaten on their own or with rice.

Ingredients

Chicken thighs (legs)	500 g (1 lb 1½ oz), boned and cut into 1.5-cm (¾-in) cubes
Shiitake mushrooms	125 g (4½ oz), stems removed and diced
Eggs	2, well beaten
Coconut cream	60 ml (2 fl oz / ¼ cup)
Spring onions (scallions)	50 g (1 oz), finely sliced
Salt	a pinch or to taste
Freshly crushed white peppercorns	a pinch or to taste
Salam leaves	8
Banana leaf wrappers	8, each about 25 x 18 cm (10 x 7 in)

Spice Paste

Garlic	30 g (1 oz), peeled and sliced
Shallots	50 g (2 oz), peeled and sliced
Ginger	25 g (1 oz), peeled and sliced
Red chillies	40 g (1¼ oz), halved, seeded and sliced
Candlenuts	25 g (1 oz), roasted and crushed
Salt	a pinch or to taste
Vegetable oil	3 Tbsp

Method

- Prepare spice paste. Combine all ingredients, except oil, in a stone mortar or blender (processor) and grind until very fine.
- Heat oil in heavy saucepan. Add spice paste and sauté over medium heat until fragrant, then remove from heat and leave to cool to room temperature.
- Combine all remaining ingredients, except *salam* and banana leaves, in a large bowl and mix until chicken and mushrooms are well coated.

- Soften each banana leaf wrapper by either holding it over a gas flame or soaking in boiling water for 3 seconds.
- Place a *salam* leaf at the centre of a banana leaf wrapper and top with 2 Tbsp chicken and mushroom mixture.
- Take one long edge of the wrapper and fold it in towards the centre to cover the ingredients, then roll up tightly. Secure open ends with bamboo skewers or cocktail sticks. Repeat until ingredients are used up.

- Steam parcels for 4 minutes, then charcoal- or oven-grill for 3 minutes using very low heat. Turn parcels over at least once.
- Serve as desired.

Add chicken after stock has mostly evaporated. For added aroma, add kaffir lime leaves to pan when sautéing spice paste and sauté together.

When chicken pieces are evenly coated with spice paste, add remaining stock and coconut cream.

When coconut cream and remaining stock has reached the boil, add all remaining ingredients, except salt.

Note: The coconut cream will cause the sauce to thicken as it cooks. Should the sauce thicken too much, add a splash of stock so the sauce remains light. This will also prevent the sauce from breaking. Also, for a less fiery taste, do not grind the chillies in the spice paste. Instead, bruise them and add them later, when spice paste is being sautéed.

SPICED CHICKEN IN COCONUT CREAM
(AYAM TUTURUGA)

The rich taste of coconut cream forms the foundation of this lip-smackingly tasty sauce. The addition of herbs and the spice paste create a mesh of aromas and flavours that are irresistable.

Ingredients

Chicken stock (see pg 11)	250 ml (8 fl oz / 1 cup)
Chicken thighs (legs)	600 g (1 lb 5 oz), boned and cut into 2.5-cm (1-in) cubes
Coconut cream	250 ml (8 fl oz / 1 cup)
Lemon grass	2 stalks, bruised
Spring onions (scallions)	30 g (1 oz), sliced
Kaffir lime leaves	2, bruised
Lemon basil	50 g (2 oz), sliced
Screwpine (pandan) leaf	1, small, sliced
Mint leaves	5 sprigs, sliced
Salt	to taste

Spice Paste

Shallots	60 g (2 oz), peeled and sliced
Garlic	30 g (1 oz), peeled and sliced
Ginger	30 g (1 oz), peeled and sliced
Candlenuts	50 g (2 oz), crushed
Bird's eye chillies	10 g ($^1/_3$ oz), sliced
Vegetable oil	2 Tbsp

Method

- Prepare spice paste. Combine all ingredients in a stone mortar or blender (processor) and grind into a fine paste.
- Transfer paste to a heavy saucepan and sauté over very low heat until fragrant.
- Add half the stock, bring to the boil and simmer until most of the liquid has evaporated.
- Add chicken cubes and mix until they are evenly coated.
- Add remaining stock and coconut cream. Return to the boil.
- Add all remaining ingredients, except salt. Stir through and simmer over very low heat until chicken is tender and sauce is slightly thickened.
- Season to taste with salt, then dish out and serve. Garnish with a sprinkling of crisp-fried shallots, if desired.

CREAMY DUCK CURRY
(BEBEK MENYANYAT)

The robust flavour of duck is complemented beautifully in this recipe by the generous use of spices, both dry and fresh.

Ingredients

Duck	1, about 2 kg (4 lb 6 oz), cleaned
Salt	to taste
Vegetable oil	2 Tbsp
Chicken stock (see pg 11)	1 litre (32 fl oz / 4 cups)
Coconut milk	400 ml (13 fl oz)
Crisp-fried shallots	2 Tbsp

Spice Paste

Red chillies	60 g (2 oz), halved, seeded and sliced
Bird's eye chillies	2–4, sliced
Shallots	100 g (3 1/2 oz), peeled and sliced
Garlic	20 g (3/4 oz), peeled and sliced
Galangal (laos)	25 g (1 oz), peeled and chopped
Ginger	25 g (1 oz), peeled and sliced
Lesser galangal (kencur)	20 g (3/4 oz), washed and sliced
Turmeric	35 g (1 oz), peeled and sliced
Candlenuts	15 g (1/2 oz)
Dried prawn (shrimp) paste (terasi)	1/2 tsp
Coriander seeds	1/2 tsp, crushed
Freshly crushed black pepper	1/4 tsp
Grated nutmeg	1/4 tsp
Cloves	2
Coconut or vegetable oil	2 Tbsp
Lemon grass	2 stalks, bruised and knotted
Salam leaves	2

Mix duck pieces with one-third of the spice paste. Make sure each piece is evenly coated.

Sauté remaining two-thirds of spice paste until fragrant before adding duck.

Begin with half the stock and simmer until duck is cooked. Regularly check liquid level during cooking and add more stock as it reduces.

Note: For no other reason except adding texture to the overall dish, add a few peeled shallots and cloves of garlic and shallots when simmering the duck. If you happen to have some East Javanese Red Spice Paste pre-made and frozen, use it instead of preparing the spice paste here to save time.

Method

- Cut duck into 12 pieces and set aside.
- Prepare spice paste. Combine all ingredients, except lemon grass and salam leaves, in a blender (processor) and grind coarsely.
- Transfer blended ingredients to a heavy saucepan. Add remaining spice paste ingredients, 125 ml (4 fl oz / 1/2 cup) water and a pinch of salt or to taste. Simmer over medium heat for 1 hour or until all the liquid has evaporated and paste is golden. Remove from heat and leave to cool completely before using.
- Mix duck with one-third of the spice paste and refrigerate or set aside in a cool place for 1 hour to marinate.
- Heat oil in a stewing pan and sauté remaining spice paste until fragrant.
- Add duck and continue to sauté until meat changes colour.
- Add half the stock or just enough to cover duck pieces. Bring to the boil, reduce heat and simmer until meat is cooked. Regularly check liquid level and add more stock as it evaporates during cooking.
- Continue until duck is tender to your liking, adding coconut milk near the end. When sauce has reduced to a creamy consistency, adjust seasoning to taste and dish out.
- Garnish as desired with crisp-fried shallots and serve.

Saté with Sweet Soy Marinade (*Sate Manis*)

Beef Braised in Coconut Milk (*Rendang Sapi*)

Ox Tongue in Sweet Nutmeg Sauce (*Semur Lidah*)

Beef Stew in Black Nut Sauce (*Rawon*)

Lamb Stew with Spices (*Gulai Bagar*)

Braised Lamb Shanks in Spiced Coconut Sauce
(*Kaki Kambing*)

Pork and Red Kidney Bean Stew (*Sop Brenebon*)

Grilled Pork Ribs with Sautéed Vegetables
(*Babi Panggang Sayuran*)

Prepare spice paste by grinding all ingredients, except sweet soy sauce, finely.

When spice paste ingredients have been ground to a fine paste, mix in sweet soy sauce.

Thread marinated meat of choice or soy bean cakes onto pre-soaked skewers for grilling.

Step-By-Step

SATÉ WITH SWEET SOY MARINADE *(SATE MANIS)*

Choose only one type of meat or soy bean cakes when preparing this recipe. If more is desired, increase spice paste quantities accordingly.

Ingredients

Leg of lamb	600 g (1 lb 5 oz), cut into 1.5-cm ($^3/_4$-in) cubes; or
Beef tenderloin or top round (topside)	600 g (1 lb 5 oz), cut into 1.5-cm ($^3/_4$-in) cubes; or
Chicken breast	600 g (1 lb 5 oz), cut into 1.5-cm ($^3/_4$-in) cubes; or
Fermented soy bean cakes (*tempe*)	600 g (1 lb 5 oz), cut into 2.5-cm (1-in) cubes
Limes	2, cut into wedges

Spice Paste

Vegetable oil	3 Tbsp
Shallots	60 g (2 oz), peeled and sliced
Garlic	40 g (1$^1/_4$ oz), peeled and sliced
Red chillies	70 g (2$^1/_2$ oz), halved, seeded and sliced
Coriander seeds	1 Tbsp, roasted and crushed
Cumin seeds	1 Tbsp
Lime juice	2 Tbsp
Palm sugar	1 Tbsp, chopped
Salt	1 tsp
Sweet soy sauce (*kecap manis*)	4 Tbsp

Method

- Prepare spice paste. Combine all ingredients, except sweet soy sauce, in a stone mortar or blender (processor) and grind into a fine paste. Add sweet soy sauce and blend well.
- Transfer spice paste to a heavy saucepan and place over medium heat. Sauté until fragrant, then remove from heat and allow to cool to room temperature.

- Mix meat of choice or soy bean cakes with spice paste and leave to marinate in a cool place for 30 minutes.
- Thread meat or soy bean cake pieces onto bamboo skewers that have been pre-soaked in water.
- Either oven-grill at very high heat or place over very hot charcoal, turning a few times. Remove when cooked.

- Serve with lime wedges and extra sweet soy sauce as a side dip.
- Another serving suggestion is to serve saté with peanut sauce (see pg 27) and compressed rice cakes (see pg 91). To save time, ready-made rice cakes can be bought at Asian stores or supermarkets.

Prepare spice paste by coarsely grinding all ingredients in a stone mortar or blender (processor).

Heat oil in a heavy pan and sauté spice paste until fragrant and golden before adding remaining ingredients.

Add beef cubes to simmering sauce and return to the boil, then simmer until they are tender.

Note: Replace coconut milk with beef or chicken stock if you prefer a dish that is less rich. If using stock, simmer until meat is nearly cooked, then add 85 ml (2¹/₂ fl oz / ¹/₃ cup) coconut cream.

BEEF BRAISED IN COCONUT MILK
(RENDANG SAPI)

The delicious sauce that blankets these fork-tender cubes of beef is rich with spices and meat juices.

Ingredients

Beef shoulder or neck	800 g (1³/₄ lb)
Vegetable oil	3 Tbsp
Coconut milk	1.625 litres (52 fl oz / 6¹/₂ cups)
Lemon grass	2 stalks, bruised
Turmeric leaf	1, torn and knotted
Kaffir lime leaves	3, bruised
Salt	to taste

Spice Paste

Shallots	60 g (2 oz), peeled and sliced
Garlic	40 g (1¹/₄ oz), peeled and sliced
Red chillies	100 g (3¹/₂ oz), halved, seeded and sliced
Turmeric	35 g (1 oz), peeled and sliced
Galangal (*laos*)	35 g (1 oz), peeled and sliced
Ginger	35 g (1 oz), peeled and sliced
Candlenuts	35 g (1 oz), roasted and crushed
Crushed black peppercorns	³/₄ tsp

Method

- Cut cleaned beef into 2.5-cm (1-in) cubes, then set aside.
- Prepare spice paste. Combine all ingredients in a stone mortar or blender (processor) and grind coarsely.
- Heat oil in heavy saucepan, add spice paste and sauté over medium heat until fragrant and colour changes.
- Add coconut milk, lemon grass and turmeric and kaffir lime leaves. Bring to the boil.
- Add beef cubes and return to the boil, then reduce heat and simmer until meat is tender and almost all the liquid has evaporated. Stir frequently.
- Season to taste with salt and remove from heat when dish appears dry and oily.

Combine stock, half the spice paste, *salam* and kaffir lime leaves and lemon grass in a pot and bring to the boil.

Use a very sharp knife to remove outer layer of cooked tongue.

After removing the outer layer, slice tongue into desired serving-size pieces and set aside.

S t e p - B y - S t e p

OX TONGUE IN SWEET NUTMEG SAUCE
(SEMUR LIDAH)

This dish of ultra-tender tongue in a richly flavourful dark sauce makes an aromatic and tasty meal with plain, steamed rice.

Ingredients

Beef or chicken stock (see pg 11)	2.5 litres (4 pints / 10 cups)
Salam leaves	4
Kaffir lime leaves	4, bruised
Lemon grass	2 stalks, bruised
Ox tongue	1, 800 g–1.2 kg (1³/₄ lb–2 lb 10 oz)
Sweet soy sauce (*kecap manis*)	4 Tbsp
Potatoes	3, medium, peeled and cut into wedges
Salt	a pinch or to taste
Crisp-fried shallots for garnishing	

Spice Paste

Red chillies	150 g (5 oz), halved, seeded and sliced
Bird's eye chillies	30 g (1 oz), finely sliced
Shallots	75 g (2¹/₂ oz), peeled and sliced
Garlic	35 g (1 oz), peeled and sliced
Ginger	35 g (1 oz), peeled and sliced
Galangal (*laos*)	60 g (2 oz), peeled and sliced
Candlenuts	75 g (2¹/₂ oz), roasted and crushed
Coriander seeds	1 Tbsp, roasted and crushed
Black peppercorns	¹/₂ Tbsp, crushed
Grated nutmeg	¹/₂ tsp
Vegetable oil	75 ml (2¹/₂ fl oz)
Water	100 ml (3¹/₂ fl oz)

Method

- Prepare spice paste. Combine all ingredients, except oil and water, in a stone mortar or blender (processor) and grind coarsely.
- Transfer ground ingredients to a heavy saucepan, add oil and water and simmer over medium heat for about 20 minutes or until water has evaporated. Remove from heat and leave to cool.
- Combine stock, half the spice paste, *salam* and kaffir lime leaves and lemon grass in a heavy stockpot. Bring to the boil, then reduce heat and simmer for 5 minutes.

- Add ox tongue, return to the boil and simmer over very low heat for about 3 hours or until tongue is very tender. To check, insert a skewer into the centre and remove; it should slide in and out easily.
- Remove cooked tongue from stockpot and plunge into ice water to cool. Remove outer layer with a sharp knife, then slice.
- Strain stock into a clean saucepan, then place over heat and reduce to about 500 ml (16 fl oz / 2 cups).

- Add remaining spice paste, soy sauce and potatoes. Return to the boil and simmer until potatoes are nearly cooked.
- Add ox tongue slices and return to the boil again, then simmer until potatoes are soft and sauce has reduced to a light, syrupy consistency.
- Season to taste with salt, then dish out. Garnish with crisp-fried shallots and serve.

BEEF STEW IN BLACK NUT SAUCE (RAWON)

Black nuts or *buah keluak* are an Indonesian speciality and their unique flavour is best brought out in a thick, meaty stew.

Ingredients

Vegetable oil	3 Tbsp
Lemon grass	1 stalk, bruised
Kaffir lime leaves	3, bruised
Beef brisket or shoulder	800 g (1¾ lb), cut into 2-cm (1-in) cubes
Beef stock (see pg 11)	1.5 litres (48 fl oz / 6 cups), hot
Salt	to taste
Ground black pepper	to taste
Crisp-fried shallots for garnishing	

Spice Paste

Red chillies	2, halved, seeded and sliced
Candlenuts	3, roasted
Turmeric	1 Tbsp, peeled and chopped
Galangal (*laos*)	1 Tbsp, peeled and chopped
Garlic	4, peeled and sliced
Shallots	8, peeled and sliced
Dried prawn (shrimp) paste (*terasi*)	½ tsp, roasted
Coriander seeds	1 Tbsp, crushed
Sweet soy sauce (*kecap manis*)	1 Tbsp
Palm sugar	1 Tbsp
Indonesian black nuts (*buah keluak*)	3–4, shelled and blanched until tender
Tamarind pulp	1 Tbsp

S t e p - B y - S t e p

Cut cleaned beef into 2-cm (1-in) cubes and set aside until needed.

Add beef when spice paste has been sautéed until fragrant and continue to sauté until beef changes colour.

Add 500 ml (16 fl oz / 2 cups) stock to pan and simmer until beef is tender. Regularly check liquid level and add stock as it reduces.

Method

- Prepare spice paste. Combine all ingredients in a stone mortar or blender (processor) and grind coarsely.
- Heat oil in heavy saucepan. Add spice paste, lemon grass and kaffir lime leaves and sauté over medium heat until fragrant and spice paste changes colour.
- Add beef cubes and continue to sauté until meat changes colour.

- Add 500 ml (16 fl oz / 2 cups) beef stock and bring to the boil, then reduce heat and simmer until meat is very tender.
- Regularly check liquid level and add more stock as it reduces. Remove scum as it accumulates at the surface.
- When the last of the stock has been added, simmer until sauce is thickened and shiny.

- Season to taste with salt and pepper, then dish out, garnish as desired and serve.

Grind all the spice paste ingredients into a paste.

After adding the meat to the spice paste, sauté until the lamb cubes are well coated.

Add the stock and coconut milk to the pan and simmer until the sauce is slightly thickened.

Note: If meat takes longer to cook and liquid reduces too much, add small amounts of stock until meat is tender. Do not add more coconut milk as this will make the dish too heavy and oily. If you wish to make a lighter version of this stew, replace the coconut milk with the same amount of chicken stock. The stew will not thicken as much as when coconut milk is used.

Step-By-Step

LAMB STEW WITH SPICES
(GULAI BAGAR)

The combination of cinnamon and lamb brings about a deeply aromatic dish that is also rich in flavour. For a lighter version, replace coconut milk in this recipe with the same amount of chicken stock.

Ingredients

Vegetable oil	4 Tbsp
Lemon grass	2 stalks, bruised
Kaffir lime leaves	4, bruised
Cinnamon	1 stick, about 10-cm (4-in) long
Lamb shoulder	600 g (1 lb 5 oz), cut into 2-cm (1-in) cubes
Chicken stock (see pg 11)	500 ml (16 fl oz / 2 cups)
Coconut milk	500 ml (16 fl oz / 2 cups)
Salt	a pinch

Spice Paste

Shallots	60 g (2 oz), peeled and sliced
Garlic	40 g (1¼ oz), peeled and sliced
Red chillies	75 g (2½ oz), halved, seeded and sliced
Turmeric	30 g (1 oz), peeled and sliced
Ginger	30 g (1 oz), peeled and sliced
Galangal (laos)	30 g (1 oz), peeled and sliced
Candlenuts	30 g (1 oz), roasted and crushed
Tamarind pulp	3 Tbsp, mixed with 60 ml (2 fl oz / ¼ cup) warm water and strained before use
Coriander seeds	1 Tbsp, roasted and crushed
Cardamom pods	½ Tbsp, peeled and crushed
Cumin seeds	½ tsp
Cloves	4, crushed
Black peppercorns	½ tsp, crushed

Method

- Prepare spice paste. Combine all ingredients in a stone mortar or blender (processor) and grind into a paste.
- Heat oil in heavy saucepan. Add spice paste, lemon grass, kaffir lime leaves and cinnamon. Sauté over medium heat until fragrant and paste changes colour.
- Add meat and continue to sauté until meat changes colour.
- Add stock and coconut milk, bring to the boil and simmer over very low heat until meat is tender and sauce thickens slightly.
- Season to taste with salt, then dish out and serve. Garnish, if desired, with finely chopped kaffir lime leaves.

BRAISED LAMB SHANKS IN SPICED COCONUT SAUCE
(KAKI KAMBING)

Like many Indonesian stews and braised dishes, the sauce here is fantastically delicious. Offal and tripe can also be used in this recipe.

Ingredients

Lamb shanks	800 g (1³/₄ lb), use whole and trimmed or cut into 3-cm (1¹/₂-in) slices
Lamb shoulder	400 g (13¹/₂ oz), cut into 2-cm (1-in) cubes
Vegetable oil	3 Tbsp
East Javanese yellow spice paste (see pg 10)	250 g (9 oz / 1 cup)
Cardamom pods	1 Tbsp, crushed
Cinnamon	2 sticks, each about 10-cm (4-in) long, bruised
Cloves	10, crushed
Grated palm sugar	1 Tbsp
Lemon grass	3 stalks, bruised
Kaffir lime leaves	3, bruised
Chicken stock (see pg 11)	500 ml (16 fl oz / 2 cups)
Coconut milk or milk	250 ml (8 fl oz / 1 cup)
Salt	to taste
Freshly ground black pepper	to taste
Celery leaves	25 g (1 oz), sliced
Leek or spring onions (scallions)	25 g (1 oz), sliced
Tomatoes	50 g (2 oz), halved, seeded and diced
Crisp-fried shallots	2 Tbsp
Melinjo nut crackers (krupuk emping)	50 g (2 oz), deep-fried
Lime	1, cut into wedges
Nasi goreng sauce (see pg 10)	3 Tbsp

Step-By-Step

Add lamb to the pot, then allow the water to return to the boil before removing. This will just scald the meat.

Sauté the spices for 2 minutes or until fragrant. This brings out their full flavours.

Add just enough stock to cover meat. Top up with more stock as necessary.

Method

- Bring 3 litres (96 fl oz / 12 cups) water to the boil in a large pot. Add lamb shanks and meat and return to the boil.
- Remove lamb and rinse under running water. Discard boiling liquid and set meat aside to drain well.
- Heat oil in a large, heavy saucepan. Add spice paste, cardamoms, cinnamon, cloves, palm sugar, lemon grass and kaffir lime leaves. Sauté for 2 minutes or until fragrant.

- Add lamb and stir over medium heat until it is evenly covered with spice paste.
- Add half the stock or just enough to cover meat. Bring to the boil and simmer over medium–low heat until meat is nearly cooked. Regularly check liquid level and add small amounts of stock as it reduces.

- Add coconut milk or milk, return to the boil and simmer until meat is very tender; it should come away from the bone easily.
- Season to taste with salt and pepper, then stir in celery, leek, tomatoes and fried shallots.
- Serve with crackers, lime and nasi goreng sauce on the side.

PORK AND RED KIDNEY BEAN STEW *(SOP BRENEBON)*

The subtle flavour of the kidney beans complements this mild-tasting dish well. With rice and vegetables, this dish becomes a nutritious meal.

Ingredients

Shallots	100 g (3¹/₂ oz), peeled and sliced
Garlic	30 g (1 oz), peeled and sliced
Vegetable oil	3 Tbsp
Lemon grass	2 stalks, bruised
Cloves	5, crushed
Grated nutmeg	¹/₄ tsp
Ground white pepper	¹/₄ tsp
Pork neck or shoulder	600 g (1 lb 5 oz), cut into 2.5-cm (1-in) cubes
Red kidney beans	200 g (7 oz), soaked for 8 hours in cold water and drained before use
Chicken stock (see pg 11)	1 litre (32 fl oz / 4 cups)
Celery leaves	20 g (³/₄ oz), sliced
Salt	to taste

Garnishing

Crisp-fried shallots	1 Tbsp
Crisp-fried garlic	1 Tbsp

Kidney beans contain a toxin that may cause gastric problems if undercooked. Soaking them will ensure that they cook more thoroughly.

After adding pork and beans, continue to sauté until ingredients are well coated with spice paste.

Check the liquid level regularly and add just enough stock to cover the ingredients, or the stew will be too watery.

Note: For meats in stews to be tender and succulent, bear 3 points in mind. First, always cut the meat into chunks, at least 2.5-cm (1-in) cubes. This minimises the cut surfaces through which meat juices can escape. Second, cook at very low temperatures, about 70°C (160°F). Such low heat means a substantial increase in cooking time, so check the liquid level regularly. Third, never cover the stew as this will increase the temperature within and cause the stew to simmer and, in turn, the meat to dry out and become tough.

Method

- Prepare spice paste. Combine shallots, garlic and oil in a stone mortar or blender (processor) and grind into a very fine paste.
- Transfer paste to a heavy saucepan. Add lemon grass, cloves, nutmeg and pepper. Sauté over medium–low heat until fragrant.
- Add pork and beans and continue to sauté until all ingredients are well mixed.
- Add half the stock, stir through and bring to the boil, then reduce heat and simmer until meat and beans are tender. Regularly check liquid level and add small amounts of stock where necessary, making sure that meat is just covered with sauce but is not swimming in it.
- Lastly, add celery and salt to taste. Simmer for 5 minutes more and dish out.
- Serve, garnished as desired.

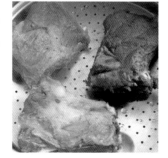

Steaming the pork ribs before grilling will ensure that they remain succulent.

Grill the pork ribs until they turn a golden brown colour.

Add the vegetables to the pan last and lightly sauté. Do not overcook vegetables as they will lose their nutrients.

Step-By-Step

GRILLED PORK RIBS WITH SAUTÉED VEGETABLES
(BABI PANGGANG SAYURAN)

This recipe requires the meat to be steamed before grilling, but the extra step taken is well worth it as the meat remains succulent.

Ingredients

Pork ribs	500 g (1 lb 1½ oz), cut into 100 g (3½ oz) portions
Shallots	80 g (3 oz), peeled and sliced
Ginger	20 g (¾ oz), peeled and finely sliced
Vegetable oil	3 Tbsp + enough for grilling
Lemon grass	2 stalks, bruised
Chicken stock (see pg 11)	150 ml (5 fl oz)
Water convolvulus (kangkung)	75 g (2½ oz), cleaned and sliced
Spring onions (scallions)	75 g (2½ oz), cut into 4-cm (2-in) lengths
Green (French) beans	75 g (2½ oz), sliced
Tomatoes	75 g (2½ oz), peeled, seeded and sliced
Salt	to taste

Marinade (combined)

Lime juice	3 Tbsp
Vegetable oil	3 Tbsp
Salt	1 tsp
Ground white pepper	½ Tbsp

Method

- Steam pork ribs for 45 minutes, then remove and cool to room temperature.
- Mix ribs with marinade and set aside for 30 minutes so flavours can penetrate meat.
- Grill ribs either in the oven or over medium charcoal heat, basting frequently with oil. When done, set ribs aside to rest.
- Combine shallots and ginger in a stone mortar or blender (processor) and grind into a fine paste.
- Heat 3 Tbsp oil in heavy saucepan, add paste and lemon grass and sauté over low heat until fragrant. Add splashes of stock to prevent burning.
- Add all vegetables, increase heat and sauté vegetables with 3 Tbsp stock for 2 minutes or until vegetables are cooked.
- Season to taste with salt, then mix in pork ribs. Dish out when they are well mixed with sauce.
- Garnish, if desired, with crisp-fried shallots and serve.

Mix chicken with spring onions, potato flour and 1 set of seasoning ingredients.

To wrap chicken wontons, bring the edges together using the tips of your fingers, then seal with egg white.

To seal wontons, dab beaten egg white on the edges of the wrapper, gather edges above the filling and press together to seal.

MEAT DUMPLING NOODLE SOUP *(BAKSO LENGKAP)*

This hearty noodle soup combines chicken wontons with two types of dumplings, making it an extravagant and a truly satisfying dish.

Ingredients

Cooking oil for deep-frying	
Chicken or beef stock	
(see pg 11)	1.5 litres (48 fl oz / 6 cups)
Egg noodles	120 g (4 oz), cooked
Firm bean curd	120 g (4 oz), sliced

Chicken Wontons

Chicken meat	150 g (5 oz), minced
Spring onions (scallions)	10 g (1/3 oz), sliced
Potato flour	1 Tbsp
Wonton wrappers	8
Egg white	1, beaten

Beef Dumplings

Beef topside (round)	150 g (5 oz), minced
Spring onions (scallions)	10 g (1/3 oz), sliced
Potato flour	1 Tbsp
Ground nutmeg	a pinch

Seafood Dumplings

Fish fillets	150 g (5 oz), minced
Coriander leaves (cilantro)	10 g (1/3 oz), chopped
Sugar	a pinch

Seasoning (3 sets)

Oyster sauce	1 Tbsp
Salty soy sauce (*kecap asin*)	1 tsp
Sweet soy sauce (*kecap manis*)	1 tsp
Ground white pepper	a pinch
Salt	a pinch

Method

- Prepare chicken wontons. Place all ingredients, except wrappers and egg white, in a bowl. Add 1 set of seasoning ingredients and mix well.
- Place 1 tsp filling onto the centre of each wrapper. Lift corners and bring together over filling. Secure with egg white.
- Deep-fry half the chicken wontons in medium–hot oil until golden brown and crispy. Remove and drain well.

- Prepare beef dumplings. Combine all ingredients with another set of seasoning ingredients and mix into a smooth paste. Use 2 tablespoons to shape mixture into round dumplings. Repeat with seafood mixture.
- Bring stock to a simmer in a saucepan. Poach remaining chicken wontons for 3 minutes, then beef and seafood dumplings separately for 2 minutes each.

Once last dumpling is removed, increase heat to bring stock to the boil.
- Meanwhile, divide noodles, bean curd, wontons and dumplings among 4 individual serving bowls, then ladle boiling stock over.
- Garnish, if desired, with Chinese celery leaves and fried shallots. Serve with *nasi goreng* sauce (see pg 10) or sweet soy sauce (*kecap manis*) on the side.

CHICKEN NOODLE SOUP
(SOTO MADURA)

Lemon grass and kaffir lime leaves give this clear soup a distinctive flavour and an inviting aroma.

Ingredients

Chicken stock (see pg 11)	2.5 litres (4 pints / 10 cups)
Lemon grass	2 stalks, bruised
Kaffir lime leaves	3, bruised
Chicken	1, about 1.2 kg (2 lb 10 oz)
Vegetable oil	2 Tbsp
Salt	to taste
Freshly crushed black pepper	to taste
Transparent (glass) noodles	100 g (3½ oz), soaked in warm water to soften
Bean sprouts	50 g (2 oz), blanched for 15 seconds, cooled and drained
Celery leaves	50 g (2 oz), shredded

Spice Paste

Shallots	80 g (3 oz), peeled and sliced
Garlic	50 g (2 oz), peeled and sliced
Ginger	25 g (1 oz), peeled and sliced
Galangal (laos)	25 g (1 oz), peeled and sliced
Candlenuts	20 g (¾ oz), roasted and crushed
Bird's eye chillies	3, sliced
Freshly crushed black pepper	½ tsp

Garnishing

Hard-boiled eggs	4, shelled and cut in 6 wedges each
Crisp-fried shallots	2 Tbsp

For added aroma, do not add lemon grass and lime leaves to the stock but sauté them with the spice paste instead. Add a few bruised chillies for extra kick, if desired.

After adding stock, bring to the boil and simmer for 15 minutes.

Place the ingredients in a wire strainer and plunge into simmering chicken soup. This reheats the noodles and bean sprouts.

Method

- Combine stock, lemon grass and kaffir lime leaves in a pot and bring to the boil. Meanwhile, wash chicken thoroughly inside and out.
- Lower chicken into boiling stock, reduce heat and simmer until chicken is very tender, about 1 hour. Remove from heat and leave chicken to cool in stock.
- Meanwhile, prepare spice paste. Place all ingredients in a stone mortar or blender (processor) and grind coarsely. Set aside.
- Remove cooled chicken from stock. Extract meat and shred finely by hand. Discard skin and bones. Strain stock and set aside.
- Heat oil in a soup pot, add spice paste and sauté until fragrant. Add stock, bring to the boil and simmer for 15 minutes. Season to taste with salt and pepper.
- With stock still simmering, separately blanch noodles briefly and plunge into ice water to cool, then drain.
- Place some noodles, shredded chicken, bean sprouts and celery leaves in a strainer and lower into simmering chicken soup for 1 minute to heat. Drain and place into a serving bowl.
- Ladle chicken soup over and serve with hard-boiled eggs and crisp-fried shallots.

PRAWN AND CHICKEN NOODLE SOUP

(LAKSA JAKARTA)

This spicy noodle soup is rich with the flavours of coconut milk and fresh spices such as turmeric and coriander.

Ingredients

Vegetable oil	2 Tbsp
Lemon grass	2 stalks, bruised
Kaffir lime leaves	3, bruised
Chicken thigh (leg) meat	150 g (5 oz), cut into 1-cm (¹/₂-in) cubes
Chicken stock (see pg 11)	500 ml (16 fl oz / 2 cups)
Coconut milk	500 ml (16 fl oz / 2 cups)
Shelled prawns (shrimps)	150 g (5 oz), deveined
Snapper fillet	150 g (5 oz), cut into 1-cm (¹/₂-in) slices
Lemon basil	8 sprigs, roughly sliced
Salt	to taste
Freshly ground white pepper	to taste
Transparent (glass) noodles	160 g (5¹/₃ oz), soaked in warm water for 5 minutes

Spice Paste

Garlic	40 g (1¹/₄ oz), peeled and sliced
Shallots	80 g (3 oz), peeled and sliced
Candlenuts	40 g (1¹/₄ oz), roasted
Turmeric	50 g (2 oz), peeled and sliced
Bird's eye chillies	3, sliced
Coriander seeds	1 tsp, roasted and finely crushed
Dried prawn (shrimp) paste (terasi)	1 tsp, roasted and finely crumbed

Garnishing

Crisp-fried shallots
Chopped celery leaves

Bruise the lemon grass and tie into a knot to prevent the fibres from separating before sautéing with the spice paste and kaffir lime leaves.

Add chicken stock and stir to mix well with spice paste.

Adding coconut milk to the soup will help thicken it while providing additional flavour and a delicious creaminess.

Note: Purchase fresh prawns whenever possible as they are far superior to frozen ones. To further enhance their taste and texture, soak prawns, with their shells intact, in heavily salted ice water for 1 hour before use. This gives the prawns a beautifully crisp texture. Also, if you happen to have some Balinese Seafood Spice Paste pre-made and frozen, use it instead of preparing spice paste here to save time.

Method

- Prepare spice paste. Place all ingredients in a stone mortar or blender (processor) and grind coarsely.
- Heat oil in a heavy saucepan. Add spice paste, lemon grass and kaffir lime leaves. Sauté over medium heat until fragrant.
- Add chicken and continue to sauté for 2 minutes more.
- Add stock and coconut milk. Bring to the boil and simmer for 1 minute.
- Add prawns and fish slices. Return to the boil and simmer over very low heat for 1 minute.
- Add lemon basil and season to taste with salt and pepper.
- Separately blanch glass noodles briefly and divide among serving bowls.
- Ladle soup over and top with chicken, prawns and fish. Garnish as desired and serve.

It takes a few hours of simmering over low heat for the beef legs to become tender, so start preparing this dish in advance.

When sautéing the spice paste, stir frequently to prevent it from burning.

Add stock when spice paste is fragrant and bring to the boil, then simmer for 5 minutes.

Note: To save time, ready-made compressed rice cakes, or *lontong*, can be bought from Asian stores and supermarkets.

S t e p - B y - S t e p

BEEF SOUP WITH RICE CAKES *(LONTONG KIKIL)*

The rich, creamy taste of this beef soup goes well with the plain-tasting sticky rice cakes, which make a great alternative to steamed rice.

Ingredients

Beef legs (boneless)	1 kg (2 lb 3 oz)
Water	5 litres (8 pints / 20 cups)
Ginger	80 g, peeled, sliced and bruised
Salt	1 Tbsp
Lemon grass	6 stalks, bruised
Vegetable oil	3 Tbsp
East Javanese yellow spice paste (see pg 10)	250 g (9 oz / 1 cup)
Kaffir lime leaves	5
Beef stock (see pg 11)	1 litre (32 fl oz / 4 cups)
Coconut cream	250 ml (8 fl oz / 1 cup)
Salt	to taste
Freshly crushed black pepper	to taste
Compressed rice cake (*lontong*)*	300 g (10 oz)
Celery leaves	25 g (1 oz), sliced
Crisp-fried shallots	2 Tbsp

Method

- Wash beef legs thoroughly under running water, drain and set aside.
- Combine water, ginger, salt and 3 stalks of lemon grass and bring to the boil.
- Add beef, reduce heat and simmer until meat is very soft; this takes several hours.
- When meat is soft, drain and leave to cool. Discard boiling liquid. Slice cooled leg meat into small, even strips and set aside until needed.
- Heat oil in a heavy saucepan. Add spice paste, kaffir lime leaves and remaining lemon grass. Sauté until fragrant.
- Add beef stock, bring to the boil and simmer for 5 minutes over medium heat.
- Add coconut cream, return to the boil and season to taste with salt and pepper. Keep soup warm.
- Meanwhile, steam rice cake until hot, then cut into even slices and divide among individual serving bowls.
- Ladle beef soup over rice cakes and garnish as desired with celery and crisp-fried shallots. Serve hot.

*Compressed Rice Cake (Lontong)

Ginger	30 g (1 oz), peeled, sliced and bruised
Shallots	50 g (2 oz), peeled and sliced
Vegetable oil	3 Tbsp
Screwpine (*pandan*) leaf	1
Lemon grass	1 stalk, bruised
Glutinous rice	300 g (10 oz), washed and drained
Coconut milk	600 ml (1 pint / 2½ cups)
Salt	a pinch
Banana leaves for wrapping	

Method

- Grind ginger and shallots finely.
- Heat oil and sauté above with screwpine leaf and lemon grass until fragrant, then add rice and sauté until evenly coated.
- Add coconut milk and salt. Bring to the boil, reduce heat and simmer, stirring continuously, until all the liquid has been absorbed. Remove and cool completely.
- Divide rice into desired serving portions and wrap in banana leaf—roll up tightly to form a sausage shape, then secure with skewers or string.
- Steam for 30 minutes or until cooked.

FRIED RICE WITH NOODLES
(NASI GORENG MAWUT)

This unusual recipe combines both rice and noodles in a single dish, but the result is simply delicious. This is a popular dish in East Java.

Ingredients

Vegetable oil	3 Tbsp
Chicken thighs (legs)	100 g (3½ oz), boned and cut into 1-cm (½-in) cubes
Shelled prawns (shrimps)	100 g (3½ oz), deveined and cut into 1-cm (½-in) pieces
Red chillies	20 g (¾ oz), halved, seeded and sliced
White cabbage	50 g (2 oz), sliced
Nasi goreng sauce (see pg 10)	3 Tbsp
Salty soy sauce (*kecap asin*)	2 Tbsp
Eggs	2
Cooked rice	300 g (10 oz), thoroughly cooled
Egg noodles	300 g (10 oz), cooked and cooled
Spinach	30 g (1 oz), cleaned and roughly sliced
Leek or spring onions (scallions)	30 g (1 oz), sliced
Celery leaves	20 g (¾ oz), sliced
Salt	to taste
Freshly crushed black pepper	to taste
Crisp-fried shallots	2 Tbsp

S t e p - B y - S t e p

Chicken and prawns cook quickly, so be careful not to overcook them.

After adding eggs, increase heat and stir-fry briskly to scramble, then reduce heat to finish.

After adding noodles and rice, stir-fry continuously until they are well mixed with other ingredients.

Method

- Heat oil in a heavy saucepan or wok. Add chicken and prawns and stir-fry for 1 minute or until both ingredients have changed colour.
- Add chillies and cabbage and sauté for 1 minute more.

- Add *nasi goreng* and salty soy sauces. Stir-fry until all ingredients are evenly coated, then add eggs and scramble over high heat.
- Add rice and noodles and continue to stir-fry until all ingredients are well mixed and hot, about 3 minutes.

- Finally, add spinach, leek or spring onions and celery. Stir-fry for 1 minute, seasoning to taste with salt and pepper.
- Dish out and garnish with crisp-fried shallots before serving.

Immediately after adding the egg and bean curd mix to the pan, move the bean curd pieces so they sit evenly in the omelette.

After turning omelette over, let it sit in the pan until it browns a bit, but do not let it become too dry.

Grinding the ingredients for the sauce helps release their flavours.

BEAN CURD OMELETTE ON RICE CAKES *(TAHU TELOR)*

The black prawn (shrimp) paste *(petis)* is a common ingredient in Indonesian cooking. It has a strong, distinctive flavour and may take some getting used to.

Ingredients

Compressed rice cake *(lontong)* (see pg 91)	300 g (10 oz)
Firm bean curd	300 g (10 oz), sliced into rectangles
Rice flour	2 Tbsp
Vegetable oil	2 Tbsp + enough for shallow-frying
Eggs	4, well beaten
Salt	to taste
Ground white pepper	to taste
Bean sprouts	100 g (3½ oz)
Celery leaves	10 g (⅓ oz), sliced
Ready-fried prawn (shrimp) crackers	20 g (¾ oz)

Sauce

Raw peanuts	250 g (9 oz), with skins intact and deep-fried or roasted until golden
Bird's eye chillies	3–5, sliced
Garlic	2 cloves, peeled and sliced
Sweet soy sauce *(kecap manis)*	2 Tbsp
Salty soy sauce *(kecap asin)*	¾ Tbsp
Black prawn (shrimp) paste *(petis)*	1 tsp
Lime juice	1 tsp
Salt	to taste

Method

- Steam rice cake until hot, then slice into rounds of similar thickness and arrange on a plate.
- Dust sliced bean curd with flour and shallow-fry in medium–hot oil until golden. Remove and drain on absorbent paper towels.
- Season beaten eggs with salt and pepper to taste before adding cooled bean curd. Mix well.
- Heat 2 Tbsp oil in a non-stick pan and add egg and bean curd mix. Mixture should begin to cook immediately at the outer edges. Lift cooked portion at the outer edges so the uncooked portions flow underneath. Slide pan rapidly back and forth over heat to keep mixture moving and avoid sticking. After 1 minute, turn omelette over and repeat the process on the other side. Colour both sides lightly but avoid overcooking.
- Slice omelette into even strips and sprinkle over sliced rice cakes.
- Sprinkle bean sprouts and celery leaves over omelette.
- Prepare sauce. Combine all ingredients, except salt, in a stone mortar or blender (processor) and grind into a fine paste. While grinding, gradually add just enough warm water until the desired consistency is reached; it should be lightly runny. Season to taste with salt.
- Either drizzle sauce over ingredients on the plate or serve it on the side. Garnish, if desired, with sliced red chillies and serve with prawn crackers.

Weigh the ingredients and have them ready before preparing to make the fried coconut cakes.

Using your hands, mould the dough into oval-shaped dumplings.

Lower dumplings into hot oil gently to avoid splattering. Cook a few at a time so the dumplings brown evenly.

FRIED COCONUT CAKES
(KUKIS KELAPA)

The combination of glutinous rice flour and plain flour ensure that the texture of these coconut cakes are light but also firm enough to hold their shape.

Ingredients

Glutinous rice flour	250 g (9 oz)
Plain (all-purpose) flour	125 g (4½ oz)
Coconut flesh	250 g (9 oz), from medium-ripe coconut, roughly chopped
Coconut juice	250 ml (8 fl oz)
Salt	a pinch
Cooking oil for deep-frying	

Palm Sugar Syrup

Palm sugar	250 g (9 oz)
Water	100 ml (3½ fl oz)
Ginger	20 g (¾ oz), peeled sliced and bruised.

Method

- Combine both flours, coconut flesh and juice and salt in a large bowl and knead into a soft, smooth, elastic dough.
- Shape 1 rounded (heaped) Tbsp dough into an oval-shaped dumpling. Repeat until ingredients are used up.

- Deep-fry dumplings in medium–hot oil until golden, then remove and drain on absorbent paper.
- Prepare syrup. Combine all ingredients in a heavy saucepan and simmer until syrupy. Remove from heat.
- Serve dumplings with syrup.

STEAMED TAPIOCA CAKE
(LEMET)

Serve these delicious cakes sprinkled with freshly grated coconut and drizzled with palm sugar syrup (see pg 98) and coconut cream for a memorable dessert.

Ingredients

Tapioca (cassava)	600 g (1 lb 5 oz), peeled and finely grated
Palm sugar	150 g (5 oz), grated
Grated skinned coconut	100 g (3½ oz)
Coconut cream	50 g (2 oz)
Ground cinnamon	½ tsp or to taste
Salt	a pinch
Banana leaves	12, each 18 x 15 cm (7 x 6 in)
Cocktail sticks	

Step-By-Step

Use a vegetable grater to grate the tapioca up finely.

Spoon some tapioca dough onto the centre of a banana leaf and spread it out slightly. This makes it easier to fold the banana leaf.

Secure the banana leaf parcel using cocktail sticks to prevent the parcel from opening up during steaming.

Method

- Combine all ingredients, except banana leaves and cocktail sticks, in a bowl and mix into a smooth dough.
- Place 1 rounded (heaped) Tbsp dough on the centre of a banana leaf and wrap up very tightly—first fold it in thirds lengthways, then fold in both open ends.
- Secure with a cocktail stick and repeat until ingredients are used up.
- Steam parcels for 30 minutes or until cooked. Remove and leave to cool.
- Serve at room temperature.

COCONUT ALMOND PUDDING *(KLAPER)*

This dessert can be prepared in advance and kept refrigerated, making it perfect for a dinner party.

Ingredients

Coconut juice	500 ml (16 fl oz / 2 cups)
Young coconut flesh	200 g (7 oz), finely sliced
Sugar	30 g (1 oz)
Almonds	100 g (3½ oz), blanched, peeled and sliced
Cinnamon	2 sticks, each about 7.5-cm (3-in) long
Nutmeg	½, finely grated
Screwpine (*pandan*) leaf	1, washed and cut into 5-cm (2-in) lengths
Condensed milk	30 ml (1 fl oz)
Salt	a pinch
Corn flour (cornstarch)	2 Tbsp, dissolved in 4 Tbsp water

Step-By-Step

Combine all the ingredients, except condensed milk, salt and corn flour, in a heavy saucepan. Bring to the boil and stir occasionally.

The condensed milk gives the pudding its white colour and adds a creamy sweetness to the dessert.

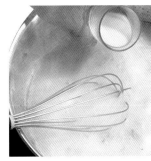

The corn flour paste will thicken the pudding without altering the taste.

Method

- Combine coconut juice and flesh, sugar, almonds, cinnamon, nutmeg and screwpine leaf in heavy saucepan. Bring to the boil over low heat.
- Add condensed milk and salt. Return to the boil.
- Stir in corn flour paste and simmer for 1 minute, stirring continuously. Remove from heat when mixture thickens.
- Divide mixture among individual serving glasses and refrigerate until set.
- Serve chilled and garnished, if desired, with cinnamon sticks and sprigs of mint.

The screwpine leaves impart a subtle but lovely fragrance to the mung bean paste.

While simmering the mung beans, check that the liquid does not dry out before the mung beans are cooked. Add water as neccessary.

Spoon a portion of mung bean paste onto the centre of the flattened dough and enlose. Do not put too much filling or it will be hard to seal.

S t e p - B y - S t e p

MUNG BEAN DOUGHNUTS
(ONDE-ONDE)

The sesame seeds coating the mung bean balls become very fragrant when fried, making this dessert irresistible and a wonderful treat.

Ingredients

Rice flour	100 g (3¹/₂ oz)
Tapioca (cassava) flour	50–70 g (2–2¹/₂ oz)
Coconut milk	130 ml (4 fl oz / ¹/₂ cup)
Salt	a pinch
White sesame seeds	75 g (2¹/₂ oz / ¹/₂ cup)
Cooking oil for deep-frying	

Filling

Mung (green) beans	100 g (3¹/₂ oz), soaked in water overnight and drained before use
Sugar	50 g (2 oz)
Coconut milk	100 ml (3¹/₂ fl oz)
Screwpine (*pandan*) leaf	1, washed and cut into pieces
Salt	a pinch

Method

- Combine both flours, coconut milk and salt in a large bowl. Mix into a smooth dough. Set aside.
- Prepare filling. Combine all ingredients in a heavy saucepan, bring to the boil and simmer until beans are soft. While simmering, check liquid level frequently and add water, if necessary.
- When beans are soft and all the liquid has evaporated, transfer to a stone mortar or blender (processor) and grind into a very smooth paste. Divide paste into 20 g (³/₄ oz) portions.
- Divide dough into 40 g (1¹/₄ oz) portions, then use your hands to pull or press each one out into an evenly thick round about 7 cm (3 in) in diameter.
- Place a portion of bean paste on the centre of each round, gather edges and shape into a ball.
- Roll balls in sesame seeds until evenly coated, then deep-fry in preheated oil at 160°C (325°F) until golden brown.
- Drain well and serve.

Make a well in the middle of the combined flours and sugar and pour the water in, then mix into a dough. Add colouring as desired.

Using your hands, shape the dough into small, round dumplings.

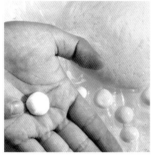

Place the dumplings into salted water to cook. The dumplings are ready when they float.

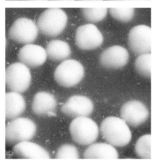

Step-By-Step

DUMPLINGS IN SWEET GINGER SOUP *(ANGSLE)*

The starchiness of this rich combination of toppings and dumplings is balanced by the aroma and flavour of ginger in the sweet soup.

Ingredients

Water	1 litre (32 fl oz / 4 cups)
Ginger	100 g (3½ oz), peeled, sliced and bruised
Sugar	100 g (3½ oz)
Salt	a pinch
Coconut milk	500 ml (16 fl oz / 2 cups)

Sweet Dumplings

Glutinous rice flour	160 g (5½ oz)
Tapioca (cassava) flour	45 g (1½ oz)
Water	160 ml (5½ fl oz)
Sugar	40 g (1¼ oz)
Green food colouring (optional)	2 drops

Garnishing

Green (mung) beans	50 g (2 oz), cooked
Cooked sago	25 g (1 oz)
Cooked glutinous rice	50 g (2 oz)
White sliced bread	50 g (2 oz), diced

Method

- Prepare sweet ginger soup. Combine water, ginger, sugar and salt in a heavy saucepan. Bring to the boil, reduce heat and simmer until liquid is reduced by half.
- Add coconut milk, return to the boil and simmer for 5 minutes, then remove from heat. Leave to cool to room temperature.

- Prepare dumplings. Combine all ingredients in a large bowl and mix into a smooth, soft dough.
- Shape dough into small dumplings and simmer in salted water until dumplings float. Drain and plunge into ice water.

- Divide dumplings among 4 individual serving bowls. Top with a little of each garnishing ingredient, ladle ginger soup over and serve.

Knotting the screwpine leaf before adding it to the syrup bruises it and helps in releasing the full fragrance of the leaf.

Allow the syrup to simmer until slightly thickened.

Should the sauce be too thin, stir in corn flour paste and simmer until sauce thickens slightly.

Step-By-Step

FINGER BANANAS IN PALM SUGAR SAUCE
(KOLEK PISANG)

As a general rule of thumb, the darker the palm sugar, the more fragrant it is. Use the best you can find for a dessert that is truly heavenly.

Ingredients

Small finger bananas	16, peeled and halved lengthways
Palm sugar syrup (see pg 98)	500 ml (16 fl oz / 2 cups)
Screwpine (pandan) leaf	1, tied into a knot
Salt	a pinch
Corn flour (cornstarch) (optional)	1 Tbsp, mixed with 1 Tbsp water
Lime juice	2 Tbsp
Coconut cream	125 ml (4 fl oz / ¼ cup)

Method

- Peel bananas and halve lengthways. Set aside.
- Combine syrup, screwpine leaf and salt in a saucepan. Bring to the boil over medium heat and simmer for 5 minutes.
- Add finger bananas, reduce heat to low and simmer for another 5 minutes.
- Should sauce be too thin, stir corn flour paste into sauce. Continue simmering for 2 minutes, then remove from heat.
- Discard screwpine leaf, add lime juice and leave to cool.
- Serve warm or at room temperature with coconut cream on the side.

GLOSSARY OF INGREDIENTS

Blimbing

Known to Malay-speakers as *belimbing buluh*, this small green, elongated fruit is a relative of the more famous yellow star fruit but it is extremely sour and is used predominantly in cooking. Blimbing *(left)*, when added in small quantities, imparts a tartness to the dish. It is sometimes also known as sour finger carambola. If blimbing is unavailable, replace with segments of lime.

Bean Curd

Bean curd *(above)* is a soy-based product and an inexpensive source of protein. The ingredient is relatively bland, which also makes it very versatile. Indonesians, who know it as *tahu*, tend to use the firm variety in their cooking. The process of making bean curd is long and laborious—raw soy beans are first soaked for about three hours and then thoroughly cleaned. Following which, they are pulped in an electric grinder, with their skins intact. Water is then added to the pulp and the mixture is boiled for about 1 hour before being passed through a clean piece of cotton cloth to strain off the solid matter. Vinegar, which causes curds to form, is added to the strained liquid and excess liquid is removed after the curds form. The curds are then pressed into moulds, which are lined with cloth and covered with a board. A heavy weight is then placed on top of the board to press the curds into the moulds, a process quite similar to cheese making.

Black Glutinous Rice

There is a variety of glutinous rice that is naturally black *(right)* and is typically used for making cakes and snacks. A popular Indonesian sweet involves a pudding made from the black rice that is served with palm sugar and coconut cream. It is interesting to note that black glutinous rice grains are only black on the outside and are white at the centre. Short and stubby, the black rice grains are considerably more expensive than the white variety and is seldom used in home cooking. In the fields, black glutinous rice looks much like ordinary rice, in that the grains on the stalks are not black. Indonesians know black glutinous rice as *ketan hitam*.

Candlenuts

These roundish nuts, known to Indonesians as *kemiri*, are a creamy yellow in colour and are brittle and waxy in texture. Used as a binding agent, candlenuts *(left)* also impart a faint flavour to the dish to which they have been added. Candlenuts cannot be eaten raw, however, and must be roasted or cooked before consumption. If unavailable, replace with raw peanuts without the shell and skin or raw cashews.

Chillies

Indonesians love chilli in their food and often use an amount that is far beyond the regular taste of Westerners. When buying chillies *(right)*, they must be firm to the touch, shiny and smooth-skinned, and the stem should be green. It is best to use chillies that were recently harvested and if possible, do not refrigerate for long periods as this will change the chilli's crisp, clean flavour.

Three main types of chillies are used in Indonesian cooking and it is useful to remember that the smaller the chilli, the more fiery it is. Always wear gloves when handling chillies and thoroughly wash hands and all surfaces that came into contact with the chillies afterwards.

Large red chillies *(top)*, or *tabia lombok* to the Indonesians, are by far the mildest and are mainly used as a vegetable or for flavouring. Their bite is as negligible as that of capsicums. Moreover, because of their size, they are typically also seeded before use. This makes them even milder as the fieriness of chillies comes from the seeds.

What the Indonesians call *cabai* are short and stubby chillies *(bottom, left)*. They generally grow to about 2.5 cm (1 in) in length and are the most used type in the country. They are usually chopped or bruised before they are added to the dish, to which they impart a pleasant kick.

Bird's eye chillies *(bottom, centre and right)*, or *cabai rawit*, are the smallest and also the most potent. Mostly used raw and served as a condiment, these tiny chillies create a raging fire in the mouth and are most likely to bring tears to the eyes of unsuspecting diners. Use sparingly or with much care.

Coconut

The coconut *(top, left)*, which the Indonesians call *kelapa*, is a key ingredient in the country's cooking, with freshly grated coconut *(top, right)* probably being the most used form. Many vegetable and meat dishes, as well as cakes and desserts use coconut for flavouring. In many Western countries, freshly shredded coconut is now available vacuum-packed in Asian stores and some supermarkets. If freshly grated coconut is unavailable, desiccated coconut moistened with coconut milk can be used as a substitute.

Coconut cream or milk *(bottom)* should not be confused with coconut juice, also called coconut water. The latter is a transluscent liquid that is inside the coconut and most refreshing when drunk on a hot day. Coconut cream or milk, known as *santen* to Indonesians, is a white liquid traditionally derived by squeezing grated coconut flesh. Coconut cream is, as its name suggests, thicker than coconut milk. To obtain coconut cream and milk by hand, first combine 300 g (10 oz / 2 cups) freshly shredded coconut with 250 ml (8 fl oz / 1 cup) warm water, then stir the mixture thoroughly and leave to cool before passing through double muslin cloth or a potato shredder and squeeze as hard as possible to extract the maximum amount of liquid. Refrigerate the squeezed liquid for 30 minutes. During this time, the cream will separate from the milk and rise to the top. This makes it easy to skim off the coconut cream, which is usually served with cakes, porridge and curry-like meat and fish dishes in Indonesia. The milk, on the other hand, is typically used to cook stews. Today, however, good quality coconut milk and cream are easily available in most Asian stores. I prefer cartons and instant coconut powder to canned milk.

Dry Whole Spices

Cinnamon (*top, left*), or *kayu manis*, is the dried inner bark of a type of tree found in certain tropical regions of Asia. When the inner bark is cut and peeled from the trees, it curls to form long "quills" or sticks that are familiar to most cooks. Although the spice is native to Sri Lanka, it is grown in most hot tropical regions that receive plenty of rain. Most of the cinnamon sold in Indonesia is of the *burmanni* species. Use cinnamon sticks whenever possible as its flavour is softer than the ground version. Cinnamon sticks impart a sweet, woody aroma that is warm and strong without being overbearing.

Native to Southeast Asia, **cloves** (*bottom, centre*) come from a tree that is a member of the myrtle family and is known to grow up to 9 metres (30 feet) in height. The spice itself, which the Indonesians call *cengkeh*, is the unopened flower bud of the tree. After harvesting, the buds are dried to become one of the strongest-tasting and -smelling of spices. Indonesia is the world's largest producer and consumer of cloves and yet cloves are seldom used in Indonesian cooking. The reason is that clove is a favourite ingredient in flavouring local cigarettes. The aroma of clove is assertive and warm, while its taste can be described as fruity but also sharp, hot and bitter. Notably, it leaves a numbing sensation in the mouth.

Coriander seeds (*bottom, left*) are very commonly used in Indonesian cooking where they are often roasted before being crushed using a mortar and pestle. Much like cumin, these grains are called 'seeds' but they are really the dried fruit of the plant. The flavour of coriander is delicate yet complex, with hints of pepper, mint and lemon. The Indonesian variety of coriander, which is known locally as *ketumbar*, is no different from the spice known by the same name and used in the West.

Known to the Indonesians as *merica* or *lada*, **pepper** can be said to be the backbone of the historical spice trade. Black peppercorns (*top, right*), when cracked, have a hot biting taste that is more intense than that of white peppercorns (*bottom, right*). White pepper is also less aromatic. Peppercorns in general lose their aroma and flavour quite quickly after they have been cracked open, crushed or ground, so it is best to buy the dried whole berries and grind them in a pepper mill or crush them in a mortar, as needed.

Dried Prawn (Shrimp) Paste

Known to Indonesians as *trasi* and to Malaysians as *belacan*, dried prawn (shrimp) paste *(below)* is a pungent condiment sold in small packages in Asian stores and some supermarkets. It should be grilled or roasted in a dry pan before use to neutralise the strong fishy flavour. Roasted prawn paste can be stored for several months in airtight containers. Although pungent, prawn paste adds an appetising and pleasant flavour when used in dishes.

Fermented Soy Bean Cake

Malay speakers know this product as *tempe (above)*, which was first made in Indonesia. Applauded as an inexpensive source of protein, *tempe* is made by subjecting skinned soy beans that have been pre-boiled to quick fermentation—a special variety of mould is introduced to the boiled soy beans when they have thoroughly cooled and then left for three days. Unlike its famous soy cousins, sweet and salty soy sauces, *tempe* is not preserved and is, therefore, easily perishable. Fresh *tempe* has a yeasty, mushroom-like aroma but when sliced and fried, it develops a nutty, almost meaty flavour.

Galangal (Laos)

A member of the ginger family, galangal *(right, bottom)*, or greater galangal as it is botanically known, has a strong, pungent taste resembling a mixture of pepper and ginger. Its flesh is a pale yellow and fibrous. The rhizome, commonly used in all parts of Indonesia, must be peeled and sliced before use. If unavailable fresh in Asian shops, it is best to substitute with water-packed slices of galangal sold in jars. When purchased fresh, wash galangal thoroughly, then wrap with a damp cloth before placing in an airtight container or bag. Stored this way, it can be kept fresh for up to two weeks, if refrigerated.

Garlic

Indonesians call garlic *(right)* *bawang puthi* and the variety used is very much similar to Western garlic, except that the cloves are usually smaller. Their flavour is also slightly less pungent and sharp. Try to purchase young garlic with firm heads that are free of bruises. To peel garlic easily, crush each clove lightly with the flat blade of a heavy knife or cleaver first. This makes it very easy to remove the skin.

Ginger

Widely used in Indonesian cooking, the rhizome has a thin brown skin and bright yellow flesh. Ginger *(above)*, which is known to Indonesians as *jahe*, has been grown in tropical Asia since ancient times. It was also one of the earliest spices exported from the jungles of Southeast Asia. When buying the ginger roots, look out for plump and firm ones. Ginger must always be peeled before use. It is then either sliced or pounded. Ginger is easily available in most Asian stores or supermarkets. Ground ginger should never be used as a substitute.

Lime

A small green citrus fruit, the kaffir lime, *jeruk purut* to the Indonesians, is often used in small quantities in Indonesia to flavour and marinate fish, meat and vegetables. It is also an important ingredient in traditional medicine. The fruit has a marked protrusion on one end and its skin is knobby. It has a sour and bitterish taste and is preferred by Indonesian cooks to any other type of lime. If unavailable, the common lime, which is found in most Asian shops, makes an acceptable substitute.

The leaves of the kaffir lime plant are sometimes called 'double lime leaves' because of the way they grow on the branches. These aromatic leaves are often used whole and bruised in soups and sauces or very finely chopped and shredded for fish, duck and chicken dishes.

Lemon Basil

This delicate spice is true to its name, in that it has a very pleasant lemon-basil flavour. Known to the Malay-speakers as *daun selasih* or *kemangi*, it is most commonly used in fish-based dishes where the fish is wrapped in banana leaves and cooked by steaming or grilling. If used in stove-cooked dishes, lemon basil *(above)* should be bruised to release its fragrance and then added towards the end of cooking to best retain the clean, lemony fragrance. Regular basil can be used as a substitute.

Lemon Grass

Lemon grass *(below)*, or *sere* to the Indonesians, comes in the form of smooth stalks that are faintly yellow and green. It has a refreshingly clean and citrusy flavour but is quite fibrous. There are two main ways of using it. Typically, stalks of lemon grass are bruised to release their fragrance before they are added to liquid-based dishes such as curries or stews. Some cooks prefer to knot the bruised stalks to prevent the fibres from separating during cooking. In these instances, lemon grass is not eaten and may be discarded before serving. When they are tender enough to be eaten, they are finely sliced and added directly to such dishes as tossed salads. Look for smooth, firm stalks when buying. They should not be wrinkled or dry. Fresh lemon grass will keep for 2–3 weeks, if wrapped in plastic and refrigerated. If unavailable, substitute with lemon or lime zests, which must be added to the dish at the end of the cooking process because prolonged cooking causes them to impart a bitter taste.

Palm Sugar

Known as *gula merah* or *gula Jawa* to the locals, palm sugar *(above)* is sold in cylindrical blocks or round cakes. Palm sugar is made from the sap of certain palm trees, including the sugar and lontar palms. Specifically, the sap is extracted from the unopened flower buds and boiled until it is reduced to a syrupy consistency. The syrup is then poured into coconut shells or bamboo segments to set and harden. The same liquid, if fermented and distilled, is also used to produce palm wine or *arak*.

Salam Leaf

The *salam* leaf *(below)*, or *don salam*, to the Indonesians is used to flavour a large variety of soups, stews, sauces, fish and meat dishes. Although it is similar to the bay leaf in use and appearance, they come from a completely different plant species and should not be used as a substitute for each other. Instead omit the ingredient from the recipe altogether. *Salam* leaves are sometimes labelled 'Indonesian bay leaves' by some suppliers.

Lesser Galangal

Lesser galangal or fresh zedoary (*kaemferia galanga*) is what the Indonesians call *kencur* and Malaysians call *cekur*. The rhizome is small with a thin brown skin and lemon-coloured flesh. Its flavour is unique and pungent, one similar to camphor. Use sparingly as its strong aroma can overpower the dish. Of all the spices used in Indonesian cooking, this is probably the most difficult to obtain in the West. If unavailable, use equal parts of ginger and galangal to replace the given quantity in a recipe.

Peanuts (Groundnuts)

When buying raw peanuts *(above)*, look for those with their skins still on. This is because peanuts that have been deep-fried or roasted with their skins on are tastier and more flavoursome. If unavailable raw, then replace with peanuts that have been roasted in their brittle shells. The latter variety are available in most supermarkets. Indonesians call peanuts *kacang tanah*.

Screwpine Leaf

The screwpine leaf *(right)*, or *pandan* leaf as it is better known, has a delightful aroma. Sweet, freshly floral and lightly musky, the leaves must always be bruised before use; this is to release their flavour. Purchase only crisp, smooth and richly green coloured leaves which will keep in the refrigerator for 2–3 weeks if kept in plastic.

Shallots

Shallots *(below, right)* are widely used throughout Indonesia, where they are known by the name *bawang merah*. After peeling, they are either thinly sliced or ground and used in almost all dishes, whether as part of the dish or as a garnish. Crisp-fried shallot slices make a deeply aromatic and flavourful garnish for just about any dish. Ready-made crisp-fried shallots are available in Asian stores and while they save considerable time, the ready-made variety is also less tasty than home-made shallot crisps. Indonesian shallots appear similar enough to shallots sold in the West but they are usually smaller and also much softer in flavour. If shallots are unavailable, use red Spanish onions instead.

Soy Sauce

Soy sauce or *kecap* to the Indonesians come in two main types—sweet and salty *(right)*. Sweet soy sauce is also known as *kecap manis* and salty soy sauce *kecap asin*. The salty version is made by allowing a variety of mould to grow on cooked soy beans for about one week, and then leaving the mouldy mass to ferment for 2–20 weeks. Once fermented, the mixture is boiled for 4–5 hours before it is strained and the solid ingredients are discarded. To make sweet soy sauce, palm sugar and a variety of spices— among them galangal, lime, fennel, coriander and garlic—are added to the fermented beans just before the boiling process.

Tamarind

The tamarind pulp *(asam Jawa)* used in cooking is derived from inside the large, dark brown pods *(right)* that grow from the tamarind tree. The pods are allowed to ripen on the tree before they are plucked or harvested and then cracked open so that the fleshy pulp inside can be extracted. The pulp, which is sour-tasting, also contains a lot of hard brown, disc-like seeds. To obtain tamarind juice, soak pulp with seeds in lukewarm water for 15 minutes before straining. Reserve the brown liquid and discard the solid ingredients. Some stores sell pure tamarind pulp, which is free of broken bits of pod and seeds. If unavailable, replace with a generous squeeze of lime juice instead.

Turmeric

Known as *kunyit* to Malay-speakers and "yellow ginger" to some others, turmeric *(left)* is the rhizome of an attractive perennial plant, with large, lily-like leaves and yellow flowers. Turmeric is a member of the ginger family and, like ginger, its brownish skin must be scraped or peeled off before use. In the case of turmeric, the flesh underneath is a distinctive bright orange–yellow. If fresh turmeric is unavailable, use 1–1½ Tbsp ground turmeric for every 100 g (3½ oz) of fresh roots called for in a recipe. In the northern parts of Indonesia, finely sliced turmeric leaves are used as a seasoning in many dishes. For turmeric juice, combine 130 g (4½ oz / 1 cup) chopped fresh turmeric with 250 ml (8 fl oz / 1 cup) warm water in a stone mortar or (blender) processor and grind until very fine, then pass through a sieve to strain or squeeze using clean kitchen cloth.

INDEX